A YEAR
OF ABSENCE

JESSICA REDMOND

Elva Resa * Saint Paul

A Year of Absence: Six women's stories of courage, hope, and love
© 2005 by Jessica Redmond
All rights reserved.

Library of Congress Cataloging-in-Publication Data

Redmond, Jessica, 1973-
    A year of absence: six women's stories of courage, hope, and love / Jessica Redmond.
        p. cm.
    Summary: "[Profiles six women whose husbands, all members of the US Army's First Armored Division based in Germany, deploy to Iraq in April 2003]"—Provided by publisher.
    ISBN-13: 978-0-9657483-1-5 (hardcover)
    ISBN-10: 0-9657483-1-6 (hardcover)
    ISBN-13: 978-0-9657483-2-2 (pbk.)
    ISBN-10: 0-9657483-2-4 (pbk.)
    1. Army spouses—United States. 2. United States. Army—Military life. 3. Iraq War, 2003- 4. Wives—Effect of husband's employment on—United States. 5. United States. Army. Armored Division, 1st. I. Title.
    U766.R44 2005
    956.7044'31—dc22
                                    2005023387

Printed in United States of America. Set in Minion Pro.
 2 3 4 5 6 7 8 9 10

Selections from the *Stars and Stripes,* a Department of Defense publication, used with permission © 2003 and 2004 *Stars and Stripes.*

All other quotations used with permission from respective copyright holders.

Elva Resa Publishing http://www.elvaresa.com

For the family members of deployed servicemen and servicewomen.

AUTHOR'S NOTE

On April 26, 2003, my husband, Jon, left our home in Baumholder, Germany to deploy to Iraq. It would be another three months before I would begin researching this book, months that I spent very much like the women in *A Year of Absence*. Their stories, and all the stories of family members waiting anxiously for a loved one to return home from war, share a common thread. The individual experiences and reactions may differ, but the emotions—fear, loneliness, loss, stress, pride, and even some resentment—are universal.

I began writing this book because I wanted to better understand what was going on around me: families suddenly struggling with single parenthood; unasked for and all too often overwhelming independence thrust onto the shoulders of young brides; children learning to crawl, walk, and even talk in the absence of one parent. It was the other side of the story we saw on the nightly news, and it was a story that was all too often overlooked.

The family members of deployed soldiers from Baumholder endured all the fear, stress, and uncertainty that soldiers' families everywhere are forced to endure, but without the emotional support and many of the conveniences they would have benefited from had they been in their home country. Work opportunities in Baumholder were scarce, leaving most spouses to become stay-at-home moms by default. Although some spouses returned to the U.S., most remained in Germany, unwilling to further disrupt their children's routines or to leave the support of the military community. Many hoped that their husbands would be home within six or seven months, and they wanted to be sure that whenever the soldiers did return, they would have a family to come home to.

As I, along with my friends and peers, marked the days off my calendar and waited for my husband to come home, I began to wonder how other spouses were getting through the stressful, lonely ordeal. How did a young woman with two small children suddenly learn to juggle all the various pressures of single motherhood? What effect did the extended separation have on couples whose marriages were already on the rocks? For those spouses who were coping well with the deployment, what was it about them or their experience that allowed them to do so? For those family members who were struggling, what was it that became unbearable? Isolation? Fear? Would the strain of an almost 15-month deployment result in soldiers leaving the Army in droves?

Using a network of support and information sharing called family readiness groups, I described the book I wanted to write to Army spouses in the community, and the response was overwhelming. Within only two days, I received more than fifty emails from women wanting to participate. No one, they said, had ever asked for their opinion before, and they were excited that finally someone wanted to listen to what they had to say. Some wanted to vent and complain, treating the interviews as informal therapy sessions. Most, however, simply wanted to share what the months alone had been like for them, hoping that their experiences might be helpful to the next person to walk in their shoes.

A Year of Absence sets out to present an accurate picture of what life was like on this Army post between April 2003 and August 2004. It does not encompass a single, universal experience or perspective, but rather offers these women's stories as a glimpse into the lives of real military families struggling to adjust to life during one of the longest and largest deployments since Vietnam. I have intentionally left any conclusions these accounts may lead to up to the reader.

The stories in this book are based on ongoing interviews with the featured women and other community members. The majority of the dialogue comes either from an event or discussion that

I witnessed personally or an anecdote that was later reported to me. It should be noted, however, that because a number of interviews took place days, weeks, and occasionally months after the fact, some dialogue has been reconstructed. Also, a small number of scenes and time sequences have been slightly altered or abridged in order to preserve narrative fluidity. In both cases, these devices were employed only when necessary to provide the reader with a more complete understanding of the events and emotions at play at the time.

Readers may wonder why the spouses followed in this book are all women, and it is worth noting that while it is common to find deployed female soldiers with male spouses in today's military, that was not the norm in this particular community, which is comprised primarily of all-male combat units. Therefore the primary, although not exclusive, focus of this book is on the female spouses who comprised the bulk of Baumholder's community during the deployment.

Each of the women interviewed for this book volunteered to share her story, and each had the consent of her husband and family members. In order to protect their privacy, the women asked that their names as well the names of their husbands and children be changed. The names of these six women and their family members are pseudonyms. All other names are real unless otherwise noted.

In biweekly interviews conducted while researching this book, I developed tremendous respect for each of these women, women who fought courageously to hold their marriages, their families, and often themselves together for 15 long months. If there is one overarching theme of this book, it is their ability to persevere and find meaning in what was, for most of them, the most difficult period of their lives. I am profoundly grateful for the time, honesty, and bravery it took to open up their lives to me and to readers. It has been an honor to know each one of them.

— *Jessica Redmond*

THE WOMEN

BETH MARSHALL

Beth arrived in Baumholder just weeks before the deployment. Her husband, Doug, is a specialist (E-4) who enlisted in the Army after serving in the National Guard. The couple met during Beth's senior year of high school in Michigan and got married two years later while she attended college in Arizona. Beth is a stay-at-home mom, although she is currently completing an online MBA from the University of Phoenix. She is 26 years old. She and Doug have been married for six years and have a two-year-old daughter named Kathryn.

TERESA MURPHY

Teresa, a 26-year-old Mexican-American from Southern California, met her husband, Danny, in their sophomore year of high school. They dated throughout high school and college. Baumholder is their second duty station as a married couple. Teresa works in the Education Center on post and is pursuing a master's degree in human relations. Danny is a lieutenant (O-2) and is currently serving as a platoon leader in an infantry company. They have been married for two years and have no children.

JENA RICE

Jena, a 22-year-old from Alabama, arrived in Baumholder less than one year before the start of the deployment, just after her husband's completion of basic training. She met her husband, Adam, while she was in high school, and got married soon after high school graduation. Adam, a private first class (E-3) in the infantry, enlisted in the Army in response to the September 11th attacks. They have been married for three years and have no children.

TASHA WASHINGTON

Tasha Washington, a 41-year-old African-American, grew up in rural North Carolina and enlisted in the Army after high school. She has a 15-year-old daughter, Keisha, from a previous relationship. She met and married her husband, Anthony, while she was in her late thirties and still working in military intelligence. Anthony, a staff sergeant (E-6) several years Tasha's junior, has been in the infantry for 11 years. Fearing that a heavy deployment schedule would result in simultaneous deployments, Tasha retired from the Army before coming to Baumholder.

Tasha's, Jena's, and Teresa's husbands belong to the same company.

KRISTINA HUDSON

Kristina is a 22-year-old German who grew up in a town roughly an hour's drive from Baumholder. She met her husband, Scott, a sergeant (E-5), through mutual friends soon after his arrival in Germany. They have been married for three years and have a two-year-old daughter named Marie and a newborn son named Tyler.

DIANE ARNOLD

Diane, a 38-year-old from Texas, works fulltime as a sorter in the community mailroom. She and her husband, Thomas, a sergeant (E-5), have been married for 11 years, during which time Thomas has been in and out of the Army. They have two children: Brian, age 8, and Michael, age 3.

Diane's and Kristina's husbands belong to the same company.

ORDERS

"My fellow Americans, at this hour, American and coalition forces are in the early stages of military operations in Iraq, to free its people and to defend the world from grave danger.... I know that the families of our military are praying that all those who serve will return safely and soon. Millions of Americans are praying with you for the safety of your loved ones and for the protection of the innocent. For your sacrifice, you have the gratitude and respect of the American people. And you can know that our forces will be coming home as soon as their work is done."

—President George W. Bush
in a speech from the Oval Office,
March 19, 2003

CHAPTER ONE

"There is no way I can stand here in front of you and guarantee you that each and every one of us will come back alive. I can't do that....The enemy is resisting. We will have to fight him and we'll have to kill him. But the one thing I can guarantee you is that every one of you will come back....We may not come back alive, but we'll come back."

— *Major General Ricardo Sanchez*
in a speech delivered to soldiers
from the First Armored Division in Baumholder
as they prepared to deploy to Iraq, April 15, 2003

365 DAYS OR UNTIL MISSION COMPLETE

A young Army wife pushed her way through the crowd gathered at Baumholder's Minnick Field. Somewhere in the mass of sand-colored battle dress uniforms and combat boots stood her husband. Lined up in formation, he was virtually indistinguishable from the 5,000 soldiers surrounding him. She searched the sea of impassive, helmeted faces below. Finally she found him, his right arm raised in salute as a trio of soldiers marched past carrying a United States flag, his elbow shielding his eyes from an unusually bright April sun.

One month had passed since the United States invaded Iraq. Here, on this U.S. Army post in Germany, talk of an upcoming deployment in support of Operation Iraqi Freedom had circulated for months, but it was the formation of 28 companies of soldiers on the soccer field below that turned that talk into reality. Within days, all the soldiers on that field would be on their way to the Middle East.

The young wife had been dreading this day for months, but now that it had finally arrived she felt a certain sense of relief. Let's just get this over with, she thought. The sooner he leaves, the sooner he can come home.

Returning her attention to the field, she watched Major General Ricardo Sanchez, the division commander, step up to the microphone. Bulky soldiers standing at parade rest flanked him, their legs splayed, arms clasped behind their backs. A few un-attended children laughed as they chased one another up the stadium steps, but the adults remained silent, searching for some word or phrase that might put their minds at ease about what lay ahead.

She listened intently as the general talked about quality train-ing and mission preparedness. The orders he had been given, the general announced, were for 365 days or until mission complete, and the soldiers on that field were as well prepared for the task at hand as anyone could be; they would serve their country well. Then the general's tone shifted, becoming cautionary, as he warned that despite their training, the soldiers would soon face challenges they had never "imagined or trained for," and that not everyone would come back alive.

The young wife stared blankly at the field of soldiers, the general's words echoing in her ears. *365 days. Not everyone will come back alive.* Her eyes clouded with tears and she turned, walking briskly toward home, suddenly desperate to be away from the crowd.

The face of this small U.S. Army post changed in the weeks leading up to deployment. As each company neared its departure date, sand-colored desert combat uniforms (DCUs) replaced standard dark green camouflage. Traffic cleared as single soldiers locked their cars away in storage, and gangs of young men pulsing with nervous energy paced the distance between barracks rooms and the food court, prowling for something to do now that television sets and video games had been packed up for safe keeping. Hamburger buns, ground beef, and steak flew off the commissary shelves as groups of friends and platoon buddies gathered for farewell barbeques. Lines at the video and liquor stores snaked between the aisles as soldiers' spouses purchased the necessary ingredients for a final relaxing evening at home with a movie and a few beers. The PX—an Army version of Wal-Mart—ran out of notepaper and envelopes as soldiers received not-so-subtle reminders to keep in touch. Soldiers pulled enormous green rucksacks out of attics and closets and stuffed them full of t-shirts, socks, elbow pads, and goggles, jamming their excess gear into already overloaded Humvees. They lifted their children high into the air and hugged them tightly, then turned to their wives to exchange hasty, often tearful goodbyes. Soldiers promised to be careful; their wives promised not to fall apart.

The young wife from Minnick Field resumed her weekly trip to the commissary, more out of habit than hunger. She had lost interest in cooking now that she had only herself to feed. She wandered through the now-empty aisles, picking up and then replacing items she would have bought were her husband still home: extra coffee, another steak. As she maneuvered her way to the checkout stand with her nearly empty cart the reality of the deployment finally began to sink in. Her husband was on his way to a war zone, and she was alone.

CHAPTER TWO

"Couples tend to react very differently to an impending deployment. Soldiers are often energized by the mission, spending increased time in preparation for departure and bonding with fellow soldiers. Many begin to distance themselves from their spouses and family members, instigating arguments and permitting less emotional availability. They spend long hours at work, focusing their little time at home on getting their affairs in order....

Family members, on the other hand, often feel torn between a desire to support the soldier and their own feelings of loss and abandonment. Family members may also begin to pull away and experience feelings of sadness, anger, and resentment. Conflict and diminished intimacy are typical."

—Capt. Glen Wurglitz, PsyD,
an Army Reserve psychologist stationed in Baumholder

LIFE AT 'THE ROCK'

When the time came to put in a request for their next assignment, an Army spouse who had already spent two pleasant tours in Germany encouraged her husband to apply for a third; that way she could continue her German studies and the family could see more of Europe. "What are they going to do, send us to Baumholder?" she asked flippantly, certain that their run of good assignments would hold. She came to regret her words when, a few months later, the orders arrived, sending the family to the one post in Germany that she knew she didn't want: Baumholder —otherwise known as 'The Rock'—home of the 2nd Brigade Combat Team, First Armored Division of the United States Army.

Baumholder gets its nickname from the heavy stone buildings that are scattered throughout post. Left over from World War II, these hulking structures give the post a medieval fortress-like air, and soldiers often joke that the post bears an eerie resemblance to Castle Grayskull from the popular 1980s cartoon *He-Man*. Despite its prized location near some of Germany's best wine country, it is not a sought-after assignment. Heavy cloud cover, frequent rain, and an isolated location make it one of the less desirable overseas postings. Adding to those drawbacks is a heavy training cycle that often sends soldiers to the far east of Germany for training missions that can last up to three months. "Anywhere but Baumholder," is a frequently heard refrain from soldiers seeking a European assignment.

The post, located in western Germany near the French border, was first established during Hitler's Third Reich, when the German government resettled more than 800 families from the area in order to build an army training base. Legend has it that the site was chosen because of its unusually bad weather; cloud cover was so constant and impenetrable that Allied warplanes would be unable to observe Nazi rearmament. It is unclear whether there is any truth to the story, but most who have spent a winter in Baumholder swear by it, citing the disappointing fact that while the sun may shine two towns over, it often disappears as soon as the post comes into view. After World War II, the base was taken over first by the French and then, in 1951, by the Americans.

The Army post at Baumholder is now home to one of the largest concentrations of U.S. combat soldiers in garrison outside the United States, roughly 13,000 soldiers and their families. But even though it represents one of the largest Army posts of its kind on foreign soil, it is dwarfed by its stateside counterparts. There are roughly 54,000 soldiers and family members at Fort Lewis in Washington State, and at Fort Bragg, the largest Army installation worldwide, there are more than 43,000 soldiers alone. Due to its relatively diminutive size, facilities are fewer and of smaller scale than many seasoned soldiers and Army family members have come to expect. Many Baumholder residents make the 45-minute drive to Ramstein Air Base several times a month to take advantage of its enormous PX, lively food court, and well-stocked commissary.

The town of Baumholder, which is situated just outside the

Army post's gates, dates back to the Middle Ages and is now mostly inhabited by merchants serving the American clientele and a rapidly expanding Russian immigrant population. More English is spoken than German, and earnest attempts at communicating in the local language are rebuffed by impatient but polite waitresses who quickly switch to English, too fluent to wait for the slow, tiresome butchery of their own language.

Like most Army towns, Baumholder's small downtown is lined with bars and nightclubs that cater to packs of single soldiers flush with new paychecks every two weeks. The clubs bear the names of familiar places—Manhattan's, Dallas Nightclub, Las Vegas—as though the names themselves might cure the homesickness that many young soldiers, overseas for the first time, often experience. On Wednesday nights, known as "Beer Wednesday," the bars are especially crowded as soldiers take advantage of the one weeknight not followed by a grueling 6:30 a.m. workout. There are a few restaurants, mostly German and Italian, an ice cream shop, a few hair salons and hotels, and a Baptist church awkwardly situated in a converted office building. The town offers few other diversions, and those seeking a greater variety of activities must drive 30 or 40 minutes to reach a larger hub.

Home, for most soldiers and their families, is in on-post rows of tall, cement apartment buildings. The older buildings are painted a dull brown, the renovated units a more hopeful pastel yellow. The housing is known as "stairwell living" because each building contains three entrances, the apartments inside linked by a common stairwell in which maintenance and cleaning responsibilities rotate from household to household. The stairwells are reminiscent of Soviet-era apartment blocks. The dingy, run-down communal hallways offer little clue as to what might be found inside the individual homes, which are often bright and carefully decorated with posed family photos and military unit commendations and mementos.

Life inside these stairwells took on a somber tone as soldiers prepared to deploy to Iraq in the spring of 2003. As they packed their bags and ticked items off their checklists, nervous family members anxiously monitored the progress of the recent invasion, hoping that it would be over before Baumholder's soldiers arrived, naively certain that a speedy victory would lead to the soon and safe return of their loved ones.

E-ZERO

Beth Marshall wiped a bead of sweat from her forehead and dropped down onto one of the many cardboard boxes that cluttered her new living room. The apartment, on the third floor of a dilapidated building a short drive from the main post, was easily a third the size of the spacious home she had left behind in Arizona. As she surveyed the cramped quarters she congratulated herself for having had the foresight to sell their bulkier belongings before the movers came. Even the little furniture they had shipped was going to be a tight fit in the tiny two-bedroom apartment. Kathryn's room was minuscule even for a toddler, and Beth's book collection alone took up half the living room.

She glanced at her watch, wondering if Doug might be on his way home yet. It was past 5 o'clock, close to the time she normally expected her husband to be leaving work, but in the brief time since she arrived in Baumholder she had learned to expect otherwise. With preparations for the deployment to Iraq going into overdrive, Doug had worked late every night for the past two weeks, and his workdays were only getting longer.

Beth decided to unpack one more box and then start working on dinner. Reaching for a box marked *pictures*, she tugged the thick tape off the top of the box and began sorting through a pile of framed family photos. There was a series of black and white photos taken of Kathryn when she was a little more than a year old, several elegantly framed wedding photos, and finally, at the bottom of the box, a color photograph of her and Doug on their way to her senior prom. The photograph had been taken soon after they met, and in it she wore a short, bright red dress with lipstick to match, her hair in a ponytail. Beaming at the camera, she looked no older than 14, more like a child who had gotten into her mother's make-up drawer than a young woman standing next to her future husband. Even now, a slender 26-year-old, Beth doesn't look much older. Her style has changed—she now wears wire-rimmed glasses and has cut her dark blond hair into a short, wash-and-wear style for easy upkeep—but her face still has the open, fresh look of a teenager.

So much had changed since that picture was taken that it was hard to process it all. She and Doug had moved from their small hometown in Michigan to Arizona, where Beth was enrolled in college, were married two years later, bought a house, and started planning for a family. Everything had gone better than she could have dreamed, except for one hitch: Doug's career.

While Beth attended college full-time, the first in her family to do so, Doug struggled for months to find work in his field. He dreamed of a job in law enforcement and eventually found a low-level job in the sheriff's office, simultaneously enlisting in the National Guard. The job at the sheriff's office was unsatisfying. The pay was low and he often had to work evenings, cutting into his time with Beth. But he loved the Guard. He thrived in the structured, mission-driven environment, and when the Guard was called upon after September 11th to provide increased airport security, Doug eagerly volunteered for temporary active duty.

When airport security was eventually turned over to private companies and Doug's temporary position ended, he told Beth that he wanted to enlist in the regular Army. Beth was more than a little reluctant. They were settled in Phoenix. They had a spacious, comfortable home. They were active in their church. She had a job she liked with the university and had recently begun work on an online master's of business administration. Most importantly, they now had a child to consider. Kathryn had been born a year and a half earlier, and Beth shuddered to think what life would be like, home alone with a toddler, if Doug were deployed for months at a time. But despite her reservations, she could not bring herself to stand in the way of Doug's goals. He had always supported her when she needed him, and had never once complained about taking over the bulk of the parenting responsibilities while she tried to balance a full-time job and graduate school. So now that he had his own dream to pursue, it was her turn to compromise.

That winter, following basic training, Doug went off to Europe while Beth stayed behind with two-year-old Kathryn, sold the house, and waited for the command sponsorship that would authorize their move. Doug had no idea where he would be permanently assigned and knew from more experienced soldiers only one place he didn't want to go: Baumholder. He called Beth from Germany to give her the bad news; not only were they going to Baumholder, his unit was on orders to deploy to Iraq that spring.

Beth and Kathryn arrived two months later, just in time to watch Doug prepare to go to Iraq. Now, as Beth set aside her prom picture and made her way to the kitchen to start a dinner that would doubtlessly be cold by the time Doug got home to eat it, her mind raced with all the things they had to get done in the few short weeks before he left for Iraq. She still didn't have a European driver's license, making anything outside of walking distance— everywhere she needed to go—completely inaccessible. They had yet to sign and notarize the power of attorney forms; without Doug's express written authorization everything from their car registration to their bank account was off limits to her. She still didn't know her way around post, her head was swimming in a sea of incomprehensible Army acronyms she had never heard while Doug was in the Guard, and she didn't even know a single person to call in case of emergency. Beth had always considered herself to be well-organized and independent, and it drove her to distraction that so much remained to be done and that as a spouse —the spouse of a low-ranking enlisted soldier at that—she had virtually no control over any of it.

"I'm just an E-zero," she had joked ever since Doug volunteered for the regular Army, ranking her position in the Army's pecking order one rung below the lowest enlisted pay grade. She tried hard to stay positive, taking advantage of the little family time they had and promising herself that the rumors she kept hearing in the stairwell about a yearlong deployment couldn't possibly be true. But as Doug's unit's departure date drew nearer and the reality of what was about to happen to their family began to weigh down on her, Beth couldn't help but wonder if they had made a terrible mistake.

TERESA'S DISAPPOINTMENT

Teresa Murphy, a pretty, petite 26-year-old known to friends in Baumholder for her feisty personality and endearing tendency toward self-deprecation, tucked her straight brown hair behind her ears and forced her lips into the shape of a smile before walking into the apartment that she shared with her husband. Danny, a lieutenant in the infantry, had been acting strangely ever since the deployment had been announced, and Teresa was having a hard time not taking it personally. He often seemed moody and distant, nothing like the easygoing jokester she had married, and it troubled her that their last few weeks together were filled with tension and stress instead of the relaxed intimacy they usually shared.

Teresa had attended an officers' wives' coffee after work that day and had made a point of not rushing home, hoping that by delaying her arrival Danny might beat her home for once. But when she entered the apartment she found that it was still dark inside. The light blinked on the answering machine, signaling that she had a message waiting, but she didn't bother to check the machine. She already knew what the message would be: Danny, calling to tell her that he was working late again.

Teresa dumped her purse in the hallway and slumped down in front of the television, flipping through the channels aimlessly until the remote landed where it always seemed to land these days: CNN. Teresa and Danny had paid close attention to the news in recent weeks, listening anxiously as the segments from the Middle East shifted from prognostications and punditry to real-time war coverage from embedded reporters. Each time they discussed the war in Iraq she and Danny agreed: The evidence that Iraq had weapons of mass destruction could not be ignored; the war was not about oil or gaining a foothold in the Middle East but about removing a legitimate threat to the people of Iraq and the United States and its allies; the United Nations would take over quickly; and American soldiers would be home within six or seven months. Danny would probably be home in time for Christmas.

A commercial came on and Teresa's thoughts drifted to more personal matters. Even though she believed in the mission and supported Danny's military career unequivocally, she couldn't help but resent the toll the deployment was already taking on her marriage. Danny hadn't even left and already it seemed like he was miles away. As a platoon leader in charge of more than 30 enlisted soldiers, Danny had been under tremendous pressure in preparation for the deployment and it was not unusual for him to work late into the evenings and on weekends. The long hours were a part of his job and Teresa understood that. What she could not understand was why Danny kept volunteering for extra duties and staying at work long after other soldiers had returned home to their families. Even when he was home they were rarely together. Danny always claimed he was too tired to do anything, opting to spend his limited free time in front of the television set or sleeping rather than going places with her. If there was this much distance between them while he was still home, what was it going to be like when he was in Iraq?

Teresa's ruminations were interrupted by the sound of a key in the door, and seconds later Danny ambled in wearing the crisp new desert camouflage he had been issued earlier that week. Stocky, with the dark hair and brilliant blue eyes of his black Irish heritage, Teresa was reminded every time she looked at him of the 16-year-old football player she had fallen for ten years earlier. They had been together ever since, through two years of high school and long-distance dating during college, and then their first posting as a married couple at Fort Benning and the arduous months of Army Ranger training. Now, they were preparing for their first deployment.

"Hey, little one," Danny said, mussing Teresa's hair as he headed to the bedroom. He returned moments later, stripped down to his t-shirt and pants, and sank down into the couch, leaning back with his eyes closed. Teresa scooted closer and leaned in for a kiss, but Danny shrugged her off. Teresa stared at him incredulously, wounded by the rejection. Within minutes, Danny's breathing became deep and rhythmic, and Teresa knew that he had fallen asleep. She observed him for several minutes, debating whether she should wake him and steer him to bed or leave him to sleep on the couch, eventually choosing the latter. She remained on the couch and silently watched him sleep.

Teresa eagerly awaited the weekend, hoping it would finally afford them some time together, but early Saturday morning Danny was once again called into work. He left with promises that he would only be gone for a few hours and that they could go do something when he got back. Noon came and went, then one o'clock. By the time Teresa heard his footsteps on the stairs she sprinted for the door, desperate to get out of the claustrophobic apartment, but one look at Danny's haggard expression told her that they weren't going anywhere. After a week's worth of 16-hour days and 5 a.m. wake-ups, he was wiped out.

"Come take a nap with me," he said, taking Teresa's hand and pulling her toward the bedroom.

"Noooo," she said, trying in vain to keep the whine out of her voice. "I want to *do* something. Let's go somewhere."

Danny dropped her hand and shook his head apologetically, went to the bedroom, and shut the door behind him.

It wasn't until later that night that they finally had a chance to spend a few waking hours together. Refreshed from his nap, Danny pulled out the blender and whipped up a batch of frozen strawberry daiquiris, a sign of seduction Teresa had come to recognize in their two years of married life. She smiled when she saw what he was up to. Danny's plan wasn't going to get them out of the apartment, but there were certainly worse ways to spend an evening, and besides, she needed to take advantage of every opportunity she had to get pregnant before he left. Other Army spouses had warned her against going through a pregnancy alone, but bad timing was nothing compared to the horrifying alternatives that kept rushing into her mind.

Teresa had no doubt that the Iraqi army had chemical weapons and that they were prepared to use them. They might not have the technology to attack the entire United States, but they certainly had the resources to attack the soldiers, and who knew what a chemical attack could mean for the family they wanted so desperately to begin.

Danny made light of her concerns. "Nothing to worry about," he had said casually the last time they had discussed the matter, mentioning what had been dubbed 'Operation Kuwaiti Field Chicken,' the U.S. Marine plan to use poultry like a canary in a mine to detect a chemical assault. "We'll just strap a chicken to the roofs of our Humvees like the Marines did and we'll be all set." Teresa had let out an exasperated sigh, and Danny had turned serious for a rare moment, assuring her that their chemical gear could be trusted and that nothing was going to happen anyway. Still, Teresa thought it best that they not take any chances.

Her period had been late the past two months, resulting in brief days of elation followed by crushing disappointment when both turned out to be false alarms. Maybe tonight would be the night. It almost had to be; there wasn't much time left. As if reading her mind, Danny handed her a drink and slid an arm around her waist. "Don't worry, woman," he said playfully. "I'm coming back!" He sounded so certain and she wanted so desperately to believe him that she decided to drop the subject, pretending a reassurance that she wished she could truly feel.

CHAPTER THREE

Baumholder, Germany – It's too bad there are no tumbleweeds in Germany.
There are days when tumbleweeds blowing across the empty streets of H.D.
Smith Barracks would look just about right, now that everyone has gone....
What will it be like when school starts? When it's Christmas? New Year's?
When they come home again?

—Stars and Stripes[1]

NO FAMILY MEMBERS ALLOWED

The April 15th ceremony on Minnick Field would be the last to take place in Baumholder until the soldiers returned home from their perilous mission. When the soldiers left in late April and early May 2003, no bands played patriotic tunes and there were no flags to wave, no stadium lined with yellow ribbons, only quiet, tearful moments as wives dropped off their husbands in front of company barracks, said goodbye, and drove home alone.

By the time the soldiers began making their way to Iraq, the ground war, which had begun only a few weeks before, was almost over. Most soldiers from Baumholder arrived in the war-ravaged country several weeks after the fall of Baghdad to begin a job that, as Major General Sanchez had predicted, they had never "imagined or trained for." They entered Baghdad in unarmored tanks and Humvees, relying on tourist maps and road signs to navigate, and took up their new roles as occupiers of an unknown and highly explosive land. And, as the general had also predicted, not all of them would come back alive.

Back in Baumholder, the change in atmosphere was both instantaneous and surreal. One day the post was bustling with crew-cut soldiers in their new sand-colored uniforms, loading up trucks, tightening bolts, running in formation as a sergeant called cadence, striding to the mess hall and food court in packs. And then, suddenly, the soldiers disappeared, leaving behind a peculiar quiet. In the days that followed their departure, the streets emptied of cars and pedestrians as those left behind stayed indoors, not ready, perhaps, to face the incongruity of an Army post without soldiers.

Jena Rice was one of those about to be left behind. The 22-year-old Alabama native stood outside the company barracks, watching soldiers arrive with their gigantic rucksacks and filter into the gray stone building. Her husband, Adam, a private first class in the same infantry company as Danny, was somewhere inside and, hoping to steal a few final moments together before the buses swept him away, she waited patiently for him to return. She passed the time chatting with the small group of wives that had assembled to see their husbands off, keeping a steady eye on the doorway and looking up expectantly each time she saw a pair of tan combat boots emerge. Adam had never been deployed before, and Jena was determined that the memory he took with him to Iraq would be one of a smiling, proud wife, not a distraught woman in tears. When he leaves, she had promised herself weeks earlier, all he will see is utopia. If tears came, and she knew they would, she would deal with them after he was gone.

The wait in front of the barracks was the culmination to a hectic day, most of the morning spent packing up last minute items and making sure the single soldiers in Adam's platoon were squared away. Even though Adam and Jena were relatively new to the Army and low in the hierarchical ranking system, they had quickly fallen into parental roles within his platoon, which was heavily comprised of young, single soldiers barely out of their teens. Jena, in particular, went out of her way to make sure that the young men who would soon be responsible for her husband's safety had everything they needed before heading off to war, both materially and, to the extent that she could help, emotionally.

Only when every young soldier in Adam's platoon had been checked in on did the couple take time for themselves. Adam called his parents to say a final farewell, urging his mother not to worry and promising to get in touch just as soon as he could. Meanwhile, Jena fought to maintain a cheerful façade, but her pacing exposed her mounting panic. Observing her distress, Adam strode over to the CD player and put on what had come to be their song —"I Need You" by Lynyrd Skynryd—pulling Jena in for a slow dance and holding her close. As a plaintive guitar solo gave way to the lead singer crooning, "Ain't no need to worry," Jena closed her eyes and rested her head against Adam's shoulder, willing herself to relax. It was one of the things about her husband that Jena loved most: He seemed to intuitively know when she had reached her emotional limit, and just how to calm her down. He would stop her from whatever she was doing—cooking, usually—and wrap her in his arms, swaying gently until her shoulders unclenched and she melted into his embrace. Usually the transformation was immediate, but this time was different; she couldn't quite rid herself of the thought that it would be a year from now before they would share a slow dance again. She struggled to shake off the distressing thought, wanting only to take pleasure in the moment and to be strong for her husband.

That evening Jena dressed with care. She chose one of Adam's favorite outfits, a dark blue and turquoise print sundress, and completed her look with a sweep of bright pink lipstick. They got to the company headquarters way ahead of schedule, at about 11:30 p.m., and found it already full of life as soldiers scurried about, collecting weapons and loading gear.

While Adam went inside to offer his assistance, Jena stood outside with a group of young wives, mostly women in their early twenties, comparing plans for keeping themselves busy during the deployment and sharing ideas for care packages.

"Baby wipes," announced one experienced Army wife who had already been through several deployments. "It's the only shower they're gonna get. Baby wipes, toilet paper, and bug spray. You can't send enough of it."

"I wanted to send some homemade brownies," volunteered a young wife, balancing a baby on her right hip. "You know, something from home. But it's so hot over there, they'd never make it."

Jena went through her own mental checklist. Adam was fair-skinned, so she had better send him some sunscreen. And she knew how awful those MREs (meals ready to eat) could be, so it would probably be a good idea to send him some snack food. Non-perishable, of course. Last she heard, temperatures were soaring well above the 100s in Baghdad, and the height of summer was still months away.

Every now and then a soldier popped outside for a minute to check in with his wife, then hurried back inside before a sergeant came looking for him. Finally, after hours of waiting, the call went out. Soldiers had to go to the lock down area to await transportation to the airfield, and all family members had to leave. Jena and Adam sneaked off to exchange a hasty goodbye.

"I love you so much," Adam said, taking Jena's hands in his. "Remember to listen to the tape I made for you whenever you get too lonely."

"I will," Jena said. "I love you, too. So much. You are the center of everything that matters to me. All I care about is you coming home to me."

Adam gave her hands two quick squeezes—their private way of saying I love you without having to speak the words—kissed her deeply, and turned to leave. Jena watched, smiling, until Adam was gone.

At one a.m. that same night, Teresa and Danny were awakened by their alarm clock. They had gone to bed early, hoping to get some sleep before Danny's early morning formation. Bleary eyed, Teresa flung her legs over the side of the bed and stumbled to the closet, where she grabbed a light jacket to conceal the fact that she was still wearing her pajamas. Danny climbed into his DCUs, and within minutes they were on their way to the company barracks. Neither said much during the 15-minute drive to the main post, both Teresa and Danny making a concerted effort to avoid topics of any emotional significance. When they did speak they filled the silence with small talk, double-checking packing lists and other minutia.

Danny had told Teresa earlier that day that once they said

goodbye, he wanted her to go straight home and stay there. It was likely that he would not actually leave post until sometime that morning, but he was going to have a lot to take care of when he got there and it would be easier for both of them if they only said goodbye once. Teresa had readily agreed, and as they passed through the security checkpoint and approached the barracks she was surprised by her own composure. In fact she had nearly convinced herself that all she was doing was dropping Danny off for yet another training mission—something she had done plenty of times before—the only difference being that his uniform was a different color and his destination was a lot farther away.

Teresa maneuvered the car around several groups of chatting wives, Jena among them, and stopped in front of the imposing, gray stone building that served as the company headquarters and staging area. Danny stepped out of the passenger side, opened up the trunk, and slung his massive tan rucksack over one shoulder. He smiled at Teresa, waved, then turned his back to her and headed off toward the barracks' stairs.

"Wait!" she yelled, stunned that he was actually planning to leave like that, without so much as a hug or a kiss goodbye. Danny dropped his rucksack and sauntered back to the car. "You're a dork," she told him as she shoved him affectionately, her brief flash of anger subsiding.

"*You're* a dork," he replied teasingly. They laughed and Danny reached for her. Teresa slid back into the car as Danny once again walked toward the stairs, this time mounting them and disappearing inside. She watched until he was gone, then started up the engine, drove home, and fell asleep instantly. She woke up several hours later feeling a little lonely, but otherwise fine. It hadn't hit her yet.

It had, however, hit Tasha Washington, a tall, 41-year-old African-American woman with closely cropped hair and a loud, authoritative manner of speaking. Her husband, Anthony, was a staff sergeant who was also waiting at the staging area.

By the time Jena and Teresa had said goodbye to their husbands, Tasha was already home in bed. She had said a quick goodbye to her husband earlier that evening, hoping to avoid the agony of watching him leave and, like Teresa, she had felt relatively calm at the time. She had smiled gamely as they parted ways, hoping to reassure him that everything on the home front would be just fine in his absence.

"I'm so sorry for leaving you," Anthony had said.

"You just take care of yourself, baby," she had replied with more confidence than she felt. "I'll handle everything from here." And then he was gone.

Tasha had lain down on the bed that suddenly seemed unbearably empty and waited for sleep to overcome her, but after several hours of useless thrashing she gave up on the idea of sleep altogether. She had to see Anthony one more time and, clinging to the slim hope that he might not have left yet, she got dressed and hurried back to the barracks. Sure enough, when she reached the staging area she saw groups of alternately bored, anxious, and comatose soldiers still sprawled out on the pavement in front of the company barracks, waiting for the buses that would take them to Ramstein Air Base and from there, the Middle East. Now certain that there was still time, Tasha sped over to the shoppette to pick up a few last-minute items she thought Anthony might want—Benedryl, a newspaper, a breakfast sandwich from Burger King—and hurried back to the staging area. Anthony went to her as soon as he saw the car pull in, but was stopped in his tracks by an angry shout from the company's first sergeant. "This is a secure area!" the first sergeant barked angrily, approaching Tasha in efficient, intimidating strides. "No family members allowed!"

Tasha glanced over at Anthony's platoon sergeant, hoping he might intervene on her behalf, but the man only shrugged sympathetically and signaled to her that she had better go. Tasha handed Anthony the bag, delivered a chaste peck on his cheek, and walked briskly back to the car before her husband could see the tears brimming in her eyes.

Suddenly it was real. Suddenly she knew that this was unlike any training mission they had ever been through before. A veteran of more than 20 years in the Army herself, Tasha knew enough to believe the commanders when they said, "365 days or until mission complete," and as if a year apart weren't bad enough, this time there were real bullets, real danger, and a real possibility that Anthony might never come back at all. Tasha's hands shook as she drove back to the apartment she now shared only with her teenage daughter, tears steaming down her cheeks in a hot and uncontrollable flood. She staggered into her apartment, closing the door behind her quietly so as not to wake her sleeping daughter, collapsed into bed, and sobbed.

ON HOLD

One week later, it was Kristina Hudson's turn to say goodbye, and she was determined not to let herself cry. She couldn't. Kristina, a 22-year-old German who had been married to a U.S. soldier for the past three years, had a toddler and a brand new baby to care for, and she was well aware that crying wasn't going to help anyone. All she could do now was figure out how she was going to get through the next year without Scott.

They spent their last night together as a family. Kristina video-taped Scott as he played with two-year-old Marie and made funny faces at their three-month-old son, Tyler. She hoped that the videos would keep Scott present in their young children's minds while he was gone, that the images would somehow convince the uncomprehending children that they still had a father who loved them, even if they couldn't remember him very well. Scott then asked for a few minutes alone so that he could leave a message for them to watch after he was gone, but after only a few words he got so choked up that he had to abandon the effort.

Later that night, once they had put the kids to sleep, Kristina and Scott sat together on the couch and tried to imagine what life would be like at the end of the yearlong deployment. "Everything is going to be really different. You know that, right?" Kristina asked Scott. Scott was going to miss Tyler's first steps, probably even his first words, and it was anyone's guess how the baby would react to his father after so long an absence. Thinking about Marie made them even more anxious. The little girl was a daddy's girl through and through. Every evening she waited for the sound of his truck, sprinting to the balcony to catch the first glimpse of her father coming home. She was never happier than when she was riding shotgun next to her father, bouncing along in her car seat as they listened to country music.

"I just hope they remember who I am," Scott said morosely.

"They will, Scott. Of course they will," Kristina replied. "I'll show them your pictures, and when you call they can hear your voice. They won't forget you." But her assurances were halfhearted. Her mind kept wandering back to Scott's most recent training mission, which had kept him away for three months. Kristina had taken Marie with her to drop Scott off at the motor pool, they had said goodbye, and then driven off. The next evening, Marie had turned to her mother in confusion, asking why her daddy had not come home at his usual time. Kristina had reminded her that they had dropped him off at the motor pool the day before and that he was going to be away for a while, but Marie still hadn't understood. She had been certain he was right where they had left him, at the motor pool not 20 minutes away. And if he couldn't come home, why didn't they just go get him? Kristina was determined to learn from past mistakes, and had vowed that Marie was going to watch her father leave this time, no matter how far past her bedtime she had to stay up, hoping that would make a more lasting impression on the little girl.

The next afternoon the whole family piled into the car to accompany Scott to the motor pool. Kristina and Scott kissed goodbye, and one by one he hugged the children, promising to come home just as soon as he could. Kristina watched as he trudged to the staging area, waiting for the buses to come and take him away. An hour crawled past, and then she saw Scott walking toward her again. The buses had been delayed and the soldiers had been told they could return to their families, but he and Kristina had already said everything they wanted to say to one another, and passed the time in an awkward silence. Once again the call went out, and they went through the motions of another goodbye, only for the same sequence to be repeated less than an hour later. The delays dragged on well into the evening, by which time most other mothers had taken their sleepy children home to bed. Kristina refused to budge, but she also refused to take part in any more painful, pointless goodbyes. "I'm not saying goodbye again until you get on the bus," she told Scott resolutely. She waited until the buses pulled into the parking lot, and then said, "Okay. Now you can kiss me goodbye."

Had Diane Arnold been more active in her family readiness group (FRG), a company-level information-sharing and support group for spouses, she might have recognized Kristina as she bundled her two sleeping children into her car after the buses finally pulled out. Diane's husband Thomas, another sergeant in Scott's company, was on the same bus, but unlike Kristina, Diane had no interest in joining the throng of women and children gathered for a final farewell. Instead, she watched from her living room window, which afforded her a convenient overhead view of the motor pool, as Thomas followed a stream of soldiers onto the bus and began his journey to another world.

Diane, a 38-year-old with wavy, chin-length auburn hair and a few extra pounds softening her middle, had been an Army wife for 11 years, and she knew enough about deployments to be nervous. This was Thomas's second major deployment during their marriage, and as she watched the buses creep down the single lane road toward the autobahn she felt deeply uneasy about how her marriage would hold up under the strain of a yearlong separation. The marriage was already on the rocks, and the deployment was interrupting the first real signs of progress they had made in counseling with an Army chaplain. Now that Thomas was going away again, all their problems would have to be put on hold. Again.

We are going to have a lot of work to do when he comes home, Diane thought to herself as the buses slipped out of view, not realizing at the time that the real threat to her marriage would come long before Thomas's homecoming.

SUMMER

"Admiral Kelly, Captain Card, officers and sailors of the USS Abraham Lincoln, my fellow Americans, major combat operations in Iraq have ended. In the battle of Iraq, the United States and our allies have prevailed."

—President George W. Bush,
speaking from the flight deck of the USS Lincoln,
declares an end to major combat in Iraq, May 1, 2003

CHAPTER FOUR

"The mission will always come first. The Army will not bend for you, so you must learn to bend for it."

—*An Army Family Teambuilding volunteer's advice for a group of new Army wives in Baumholder*

WE WEREN'T TRAINED FOR THIS

Staff Sergeant Mathew Leonard leaned back in his office chair and let out a sigh. As the family readiness liaison (FRL) for his battalion's rear detachment—the group of soldiers that, due to staffing requirements or health problems, remains in garrison during deployment—he was responsible for supporting the health and welfare of the approximately 400 families in his battalion during the deployment to Iraq. In his first few weeks on the job, the affable, laid-back 33-year-old with a thick New England accent was busier than ever.

He was shocked by how unprepared many spouses were for their newly independent roles. The Army had sponsored several sessions in the weeks leading up to deployment that were mandatory for soldiers and optional for family members to ensure that those left behind would have access to all the documents and information they would need while the troops were deployed, but somehow many of Baumholder's residents were still not ready. They didn't know how to access their financial records, didn't know how to get a replacement ATM card, didn't have a valid driver's license or know where to take the car in for service.

Staff Sergeant Leonard, who says he was "hey you'd" for his role as FRL after a serious neck injury kept him from deploying with his company, was better equipped than most soldiers to understand the plight of the women who came into his office; he was a newlywed, married to a female soldier who was now serving in Iraq. When women came into his office complaining that weeks had passed since their husbands had left and they still had no idea where they were or how they were doing, he knew from experience how that felt. He shared their frustration about the slow mail and all-but-nonexistent phone connections. He knew what it was like to face yet another week of coming home to an empty apartment, and to wake up fearful each morning that a spouse might not have survived the night. When upset women came into his office and accused him of not understanding what they were going through, his reply never varied. "Yes, I do," he would say, and he would tell them about his wife.

His role as the husband of a deployed soldier helped him to understand the emotional side of deployment, but he was constantly amazed by how poorly prepared some spouses were to manage day-to-day affairs on their own. "When my wife was getting ready to deploy," he said, "I told her, 'You're going to need 35 pairs of socks. Don't count on having laundry.' She had never been deployed before so she didn't know those things, so I told her. I would have done the same thing if I had gone and she had stayed. I would have written it all down for her: where to get the car fixed, how to access all the financial information, what she has to do with housing. I'm just like that. I would have it all written out for her just the way I would do it." But many of the soldiers didn't write it all down, which meant that sooner or later their wives ended up in Staff Sergeant Leonard's office.

It was an unexpected role for the infantry soldier. Instead of blowing up tanks and maneuvering soldiers through the woods, he suddenly found himself consoling distraught wives and making funny faces at toddlers as they waddled through his office. No one ever trained him to deal with spouses, so he was trying to figure out his new role as he went. In the first few weeks of the deployment he picked up a copy of *Men Are From Mars, Women Are From Venus* in part to help him better understand his wife, but also to better understand the women who visited his office

daily, seeking his help, advice, or, more often than not, just someone to listen for a while. In his crash course on gender relations
he had learned that often, when a distressed, exhausted, or angry
wife came to see him, she didn't really want him to *do* anything.
She just wanted someone in a green uniform, maybe someone
who reminded her a little bit of her husband, to pay some attention to her.

Of course, not all of the spouses who came to see Staff Sergeant Leonard in the first weeks of the deployment were just there
to talk; some of them needed real help. Beth Marshall was one of
those women, and by the time she came to see him, she was near-
ing the end of her rope.

THE HYSTERICAL WIFE

One morning in late June, Beth reached for the shower fau-
cet, checked the water temperature, and started to get undressed.
Two-year-old Kathryn sat in a pile of toys strewn in the hallway
in front of the bathroom, examining her mother's every move.
Beth longed for the privacy of a closed bathroom door and a long,
solitary shower, but that was a luxury she would have to forget
about for the foreseeable future; Kathryn was far too active to be
left unmonitored for even a few minutes.

"Okay, Kathryn," Beth said as she stepped into the shower. "I
have to take a shower now. Stay right where you are, okay?" She
had just begun soaping up when she noticed a strange protrusion
in her groin area. Where could that have come from? she wondered with alarm that increased each time she examined the
tender lump. She called the health clinic as soon as she got out of
the shower and made an appointment for later that day.

The doctor determined that she had developed an unusually
large hernia, probably attributable to the heavy lifting she had
done the previous day as she struggled to organize her storage
compartment. He recommended surgery as soon as possible, then
told her that the surgical ward at Landstuhl Regional Medical
Center, the large hospital serving U.S. military personnel and their
families, was closed to civilians in order to preserve all of the

facility's resources for wounded soldiers. That left Beth with two options: She could either go back to the States or have the operation in a German hospital.

She quickly considered the alternatives. Going home seemed to make the most sense at first, but as soon as she thought about it she found multiple reasons why it wouldn't work. There was no room for her and Kathryn at her mother's house; her two younger sisters occupied the only additional bedroom. There would be nowhere for them to sleep except the couch, and sharing a couch with a highly mobile toddler hardly seemed conducive to recovery. And even if they could find enough room, there was no way she could afford the airfare. Airline prices were at their highest summer rates, and she and Doug were up to their eyeballs in credit card debt already. She had hoped to use the extra money Doug was earning during the deployment to get their finances back in order. Going home now would only set them back further. Germany was her home now, and it was Doug's home. If Doug got injured, this was where he would be sent. If the unit moved or their orders changed, people here were the ones who would know about it first. She couldn't bear to think of severing the one physical connection she had left to her husband: their home.

But the most persuasive argument for staying in Germany was Kathryn. Kathryn had not slept through the night once since they moved to Baumholder and often woke up screaming multiple times throughout the night. The pediatrician Beth had seen about her daughter's disrupted sleep patterns told her that the night terrors Kathryn was experiencing were a direct result of all the tumult in her life during the past few months, chief among them a new home and a suddenly absent father. The pediatrician strongly recommended that Beth make as few changes in her daughter's life as possible. She needed routines and a familiar environment, and Beth was determined that, while she could not bring back the little girl's father, she would do everything she could to establish some level of normalcy. She told the doctor that she planned to stay.

The decision left her with only eight days to prepare for surgery, but Beth felt confident that eight days would be more than enough time to find the help she needed in the Baumholder community. Weeks earlier, before Doug deployed, she had attended an Army-sponsored information session that had outlined all the support available to family members during the deployment. There was a whole organization, Army Community Services, dedicated entirely to meeting the needs of family members. On top of that, Doug's company had a family readiness group that, she had been told, was filled with wives who were ready and willing to help other spouses whenever a need arose. Being new to both the Army and to Baumholder, she didn't have any friends she could call on for help, but she felt certain she could find the support she needed.

Beth quickly found a neighbor who was willing to look after Kathryn during her hospital stay. The neighbor had two small children of her own and was pregnant with a third, and she told Beth that she would gladly have done more, but in her current state a few days was all she could offer. Beth assured her that she wouldn't dream of imposing on her any further and contacted Army Community Services to find someone to help her during her recovery period. She knew she was going to need plenty of assistance. The hernia operation, her doctor had warned her, was going to be far more invasive than most comparable procedures in the United States, which tend to be done laparoscopically and involve only two tiny incisions. With that type of operation, most patients could return to normal activity within days. In Beth's case, however, the minimally invasive laparoscopic method was not going to be used, requiring several days in the hospital, after which she would not be able to lift anything heavier than five pounds for several weeks. She was going to need help with everything: getting groceries up to her third floor apartment, taking laundry to and from the basement washers and dryers, even lifting Kathryn in and out of the tub and into bed at night.

Her medical situation was additionally complicated by several factors. She had Behçet's syndrome, a chronic condition caused by disturbances in the body's immune system that causes exaggerated inflammation in the blood vessels, resulting in the possibility of an extended recovery period. There were also allergies to medication and Bell's palsy, a relapse of which began only days after her diagnosis.

Beth's first conversation with Army Community Services suggested that her expectations had been overly optimistic. The organization was overstretched as it was, trying to help stressed out, overwhelmed spouses cope with the initial months of the deployment. Their caseworkers already had their hands full with allegations of child abuse and neglect, rapidly disintegrating marriages, and depressed spouses. All they had to offer was sympathy and an emergency relief loan, in case Beth changed her mind and decided to fly back to the States.

Realizing she needed help navigating the unfamiliar Army system, Beth called her point of contact in the FRG, a kind, soft-spoken woman named Patty Johnson[1] who had a little girl about Kathryn's age. Together, they called every on-post agency they could think of, but each proved to be a disappointment. An Army Community Services program called Baumholder Buddies, which linked spouses with different but complementary needs, had seemed promising at first. If one woman needed, for example, rides to the commissary, and another woman had a car but needed child care for a couple hours a week, the two could swap services. But when the representative from Baumholder Buddies finally returned Beth's call, the woman informed her that so many wives had returned to the States for the summer that her volunteer bank was completely empty. Beth found a similar problem in the FRG. Those wives who had stayed in Baumholder for the summer were so overwhelmed that no one was prepared to take on anyone else's problems. Every family on post was adjusting to life in a single-parent home; it was no time to thrust a stranger's problems into the mix.

Seeing no other option, Beth reluctantly contacted the rear detachment. As a self-described "E-zero," Beth had been skeptical about how seriously her entreaties would be taken by the soldiers left behind to run the rear, and she soon found her skepticism to be justified. One unsympathetic sergeant told her that his wife had once broken her jaw while he was deployed, and she had managed to get through it on her own just fine; he didn't see how

Beth's situation was any worse. Beth chafed at the comparison. She didn't want special favors. She was not a manipulative, needy wife trying to trick anyone into getting her husband back, but she was not getting the help she needed and time was running out. Over and over again she explained her illness and the effect it could have on her recovery time, but it seemed most people saw her as just another hysterical wife trying to get her husband out of Iraq.

Staff Sergeant Leonard did not think Beth was a hysterical wife; he quickly realized that the kind of support Beth needed simply wasn't available in the community. None of the existing programs met her needs, and everyone seemed to assume that the other wives in the battalion would pick up the slack. It frustrated him that, while one of the Army's most widely touted mottos was 'taking care of families,' Beth was being allowed to slip through the cracks in the system. Everything was being put on the FRG, and when the FRG couldn't meet Beth's needs, no one else in the community stepped forward with another solution. Staff Sergeant Leonard came to realize that there was only one way to get Beth the help she needed. He told Beth to get her medical files in order; it was time to approach the chain of command about sending Doug home.[2]

Several spouses had already been to see Captain Ryan Bromenshenkel, the rear detachment commander, about getting their husbands sent home, and of those only about 25% had been deemed legitimate cases. And while Captain Bromenshenkel believed that everything Beth was saying was true, that she probably was part of the 25% who really did need her husband to come home, there was little that he or Staff Sergeant Leonard could do to help her. Beth turned over all of her medical records, cringing as she watched soldiers peruse her intensely personal medical information, but nothing she sent the chain of command reached the high threshold that had been set for emergency leave, which mandated that soldiers could be sent home only in cases of the death or imminent death of a family member. "The chain of command is always talking about soldiers being 'mission necessary,'" an exasperated Staff Sergeant Leonard vented, "but I wish they would realize that some of these soldiers are needed back here too."

On the eve of her operation, with the chain of command still refusing to send Doug home to help her and no post-operative care plan in place, Beth wrote a letter to Arizona Senator John McCain. She knew it was too late for the senator to do anything to help her out of her predicament, but she hoped that informing him of her experience might lead to an improved system for someone else unfortunate enough to find herself in a similar situation. She wrote,

> *Dear Senator McCain,*
> *I am a wife of a soldier deployed with the First Armored Division in Iraq....*
> *The reason I am writing to you is that I am scheduled for hernia surgery on Wednesday, July 2, 2003. The chain of command has told my husband he cannot come home unless I die. I am a reasonable person with a college education and I understand why it is difficult for them to send the soldiers home. My problem is that I have a 2-year-old and I will be unable to lift anything greater than 5 pounds after surgery. I will need someone to help me 24 hours a day for at least 2 weeks for my needs (shower, bandage change, etc.) along with assistance for my daughter.... I have gone through the agencies here in Baumholder to try to line up assistance. The problem is that the family readiness group (FRG), Army Community Services (ACS), and Child Youth And Services (CYS) are unable to provide 24-hour care for my daughter and myself....*
> *My father is a 100% disabled Vietnam veteran who is unable to come and assist me. My mother works full-time to support my younger siblings and cannot come. I have tried to work through the agencies and have come up short. I am at a total loss of what else to do....*
> *I know you may not be able to directly do anything, but if this is how families of military members are treated then we, the United States of America, may end up with less people*

re-enlisting and choosing to go down this path.[3] I am proud my husband is serving his country but I was told when we arrived (one month prior to deployment) that there would be assistance if we needed anything. In my case assistance is just not available for my medical care at home. I am in a foreign country ([I have only been] here 2.5 months) with my toddler, a hernia, and no idea when or if my husband will return home....

Senator McCain, I apologize if this issue is a bother to you but I feel frustrated beyond belief at the way my family has been handled in this very stressful situation...family members are an essential part of the military as well as the soldiers and not taking care of our own is not acceptable.

Sincere thanks,
Beth Marshall

The next day, Beth dropped Kathryn off with a neighbor and Patty drove her to the hospital, 25 minutes away from post by car.

"Kann ich Ihnen helfen?" the German nurse seated behind the front desk asked.

"Um...I'm sorry," Beth stammered. "I don't speak German."

"Einen Augenblick bitte," the nurse replied, and hurried off. Beth and Lisa stood at the front desk for several more minutes, waiting for someone to arrive who could communicate with them. Finally, a nurse who spoke limited English arrived, pointing them down the hallway.

Beth looked around nervously. The room, already inhabited by moaning patients, was filled with antiquated-looking glass IV bottles. The windows were open to minimize the effects of the summer heat wave, and Beth looked around anxiously as flies flew in and out of the open windows.

Patty had to get back to her daughter, so she left Beth alone with her non-English speaking roommates. For the remainder of the afternoon and evening Beth sat in silence, waiting for her operation the next morning. Left with no distractions other than her thoughts, she could not silence the unsettling, nagging fears running through her mind: What if they don't know what they are doing? What if I don't wake up? Does Doug know how much I love him? And the most unsettling question of all: Who will take care of Kathryn if I die?

None of those were questions Beth had to answer. She woke up the next afternoon, staring up at the bare white ceiling of the German hospital, trying to fight back pain and nausea as she slowly came out from under the anesthesia. She heard voices but she couldn't identify the language at first. German, she remembered; they were speaking German. Still disoriented from the operation, she called out weakly for her husband. "Doug," she croaked in a barely audible whisper. "I want my husband."

The nurse tried to console her. "In the waiting room," she said in thickly accented English.

Beth shook her head, muttering, "No, no," but the nurse did not understand, and continued to insist that Beth's husband was in the waiting room. Beth burst into exhausted, delirious tears. "No!" she wailed. "He's not in the waiting room. He's in Iraq!"

Apart from Patty's daily visits, the only other people Beth saw were the patient liaison from Baumholder —a sympathetic woman but still a stranger—and the English-speaking nurse who came by once a day to check on her. Beth begged the nurse for more pain medication, but the nurse would give her nothing stronger than Tylenol. She was in physical agony, worried about Kathryn, who had never been left alone overnight without either parent before, and desperately lonely. She longed for Doug. Just knowing that he was nearby would have been a comfort, but she had given up hope that the Army would agree to send him home. She felt utterly abandoned and betrayed. The Army had promised to help her while Doug was away, but where were they now?

Six days later, when Beth was released from the hospital, Patty picked her up and began to drive her home, but it was obvious within minutes that Beth was so incapacitated from surgery that she could not be left alone. Seeing no other option, Patty generously volunteered to take Beth and Kathryn home with her. Beth depended on Patty for everything; she prepared all the meals, looked after Kathryn, even helped Beth with the humiliating task of bathing, and although Beth was extremely grateful to her, she also felt terribly awkward. Patty was always pleasant and uncomplaining, but Beth knew their presence in her home was a strain.

The following week, as Beth lay on the couch, she overheard Kathryn and Patty's daughter fighting over a toy. The two only children had been at each other's throats all morning, unaccustomed to having to share their toys and living space. Beth wanted to get up to stop them, but she barely had the strength to dress herself, much less separate the two indignant bundles of energy. We have got to get out of here, she thought. She had no idea how she would manage on her own, but intruding on someone else's space had become intolerable.

Just then, there was a knock at the door. Patty was out, so Beth lifted herself gingerly from the couch and made her way to the door. There, standing in the hallway of Patty's building, was Doug, his bright, cornflower blue eyes smiling at her from his tanned face. His chain of command had finally agreed to make an exception to the policy and let him come home for a few weeks to care for Beth during her recovery. Beth stared at him, trying to convince herself that he was real. "Take me home," she told him, collapsing into his arms.

CHAPTER FIVE

"Anybody who wants to harm American troops will be found and brought to justice. There are some that feel that if they attack us that we may decide to leave prematurely.... There are some who feel like the conditions are such that they can attack us there. My answer is, bring 'em on."

—*President George W. Bush*
responding to concerns about rising numbers
of U.S. troop casualties in Iraq, July 3, 2003

BRING 'EM ON

When President Bush issued his controversial challenge to insurgents just two months after Baumholder's soldiers arrived in the Middle East, the reaction on post was mixed. Some, Beth and Tasha among them, were privately outraged that the president had so audaciously thrown down the gauntlet, inflaming the violent passions of an already explosive region. They viewed the remark as callous, evidence of how lightly the president took the sacrifice of both the men and women in uniform and of all those left behind, waiting through fear-filled days and nights for an uncertain homecoming that seemed an eternity away.

Yet despite their resentment, most of those who were angered by the president's charge to "bring 'em on" kept their feelings to themselves, careful to say nothing that could be misconstrued as unpatriotic or unsupportive of the soldiers and their mission. They knew that their opposition to the president's remarks put them in the minority and that most other wives on post accepted the challenge as part of the system of honor and duty to which their husbands were bound. The soldiers were, as one proud

sergeant's wife put it, "fighting for something bigger than themselves." If having American soldiers in Iraq meant that the same
breed of terrorists who had brought so much anguish to the United
States back on September 11th, 2001 would go to Iraq instead of
bringing the fight to the American public, then that was a role
they were more than ready to see the troops take on.

While President Bush's strong words had placed much of the
Baumholder community firmly in one camp or the other, Kristina
Hudson found herself in a strange no man's land somewhere
between the two. As a German citizen, she felt little connection to
the fears of terrorist attacks held by many of her American counterparts. She had no idea if Saddam Hussein was as much of a
threat as the American and British governments said he was; it
wasn't something she thought about often. Her support for the
war came not out of any political conviction but out of her unwa-
vering support for her husband and the military community she
had married into three years earlier.

Even as a little girl, Kristina had known she was going to marry
an American soldier. Perhaps it was because she had spent her
entire childhood near an American army base and, as she had
first started to notice boys, the cocky young soldiers she had seen
around town were both familiar and alluringly exotic. Friends
had warned her against getting too serious about dating the single
soldiers. They were only out for a good time, friends said, and as
soon as their time was up in Germany, they'd be gone. Kristina
had casually dated a few soldiers and had begun to suspect that
her friends might be right about them, until she met Scott.

One night she went out to a club with a few girlfriends, and a
mutual friend introduced the tall, attractive teen with long brown
hair and greenish eyes to a handsome, lanky, blond soldier. Scott
had grown up in rural Texas in the kind of small town in the
middle of nowhere that a person had to fight his way out of. He
had always longed to go see the world, but with college never in
his plans, he had found few escape routes. He saw his life stagnat-
ing and felt certain that unless he did something drastic, he was
never going anywhere in life besides a job in the local prison and
his parents' front porch. So, at the age of 21, he had enlisted in the

Army and requested an immediate assignment in Germany.

Kristina and Scott saw a lot of each other in the days after they met, and the more she saw of him, the more interested she became. He was different from other soldiers she had known, eager to travel and learn more about her culture. Unlike many other soldiers, he was trying to learn German and sought out her help learning new words. On weekends they would pick a spot on a map and go, just to find out what was there.

Before the year was out, Scott and Kristina were married, and only a few weeks after the wedding she discovered that she was pregnant. The unplanned pregnancy was initially overwhelming to the new couple, both of whom felt uneasy about becoming parents at such a young age, but by the time their baby girl was born they were overjoyed with the new addition to their family. Kristina soon became pregnant with a second child, and throughout the final months of her pregnancy she watched the news coverage of Navy ships converging in the Persian Gulf and wondered how much of the new baby's life Scott would miss.

The summer of 2003 brought record-breaking heat to Baumholder, with temperatures across Europe soaring into the high 90s and beyond, though few in Baumholder felt they had any right to complain. In Iraq, the temperatures were even higher, some days so hot that only a meat thermometer could deliver an accurate reading. As Kristina sweated through the summer heat wave she tried to distract herself from the disturbing images of roadside bombs and the burning carcasses of Humvees on the nightly news, instead focusing her attention on the needs of her two small children and doing whatever she could to ease the strain of deployment for Scott. Whenever she could muster the willpower to gather up the kids and venture out into the oppressive heat, she filled boxes with the baby wipes soldiers were using in lieu of showers, beef jerky, rolls of toilet paper, cases of cigarettes, and freshly laundered t-shirts that she wrapped up tightly in plastic so that when they reached Baghdad they would still smell like home.

Scott had been gone for two months, and during that time

her contact with him had been limited to a few brief, scratchy phone calls and two letters that Scott had written weeks earlier. At first Kristina wrote nightly, telling Scott every detail of Tyler and Marie's development, but as the weeks passed she became increasingly frustrated with the one-sided nature of their communication. She wasn't even sure her letters were reaching him; the mail system was so slow that even if he responded to a letter right away—and she knew he never did—it wouldn't reach her for weeks or even months.

Climbing into bed one miserably hot night in early July, Kristina set aside the blank sheet of notebook paper she could not bring herself to fill and clutched the phone in both hands. "Call me!" she yelled, willing it to ring. She shook the phone, choking it as if it were responsible for her husband's continuing absence, but the phone remained infuriatingly silent.

While no one in Baumholder had heard from her husband in the first several weeks of deployment, phone calls from Iraq had recently become increasingly frequent. Just that morning Kristina had overheard two women in line at the commissary laughing that their husbands called so often that they were getting sick of them, and it had made her seethe with frustration. Soldiers based in the Green Zone, the heavily fortified area that housed the American bureaucrats now attempting to run Iraq, were able to easily call home about once a week, sometimes more, but for those outside of the Green Zone the only way to call home was to wait in line, often for hours at a time, for a phone connection that more often than not was disconnected after only a few minutes of nearly incomprehensible static-filled conversation. All together she had spoken to Scott no more than 15 minutes since he deployed, each conversation consisting of the same rushed, "I love you" and "Are you doing okay? Are you safe?"

"Are you safe?" was one of the first questions almost everyone asked when a soldier called from Iraq. News of rocket propelled grenade attacks and improvised explosive devices (IEDs) planted on roads frequented by patrolling soldiers filled the headlines, and it was becoming increasingly clear that the joyful welcome soldiers had expected upon their arrival was not the greeting many in the nascent Iraqi insurgency had in mind.

President Bush had declared an end to "major combat opera-tions" May 1st, but it was clear to Kristina, along with everyone else in Baumholder, that the war was far from over. With news of attacks and combat-related deaths coming in every day now, Iraq seemed more dangerous than ever. Kristina, struggling to cope with the feelings of fear and loneliness that sometimes over-whelmed her, came to the gradual realization that the only way she was going to be able to get through the yearlong deployment was to distance herself from Scott, not physically—the Army had done a good job of that already—but emotionally. She simply could not go through every day hoping for a phone call that never came and searching the news for information that she could never verify. But just as she resolved to find some way to steel herself against the pain of deployment, Kristina had an experience that slammed her right back into the harsh reality of the war.

The phone that Kristina had been willing to ring finally did the next morning, although it was not the call she had been ex-pecting. A friend was on the line, wanting to know if Kristina could help her take her son, who had broken his ankle, to Landstuhl Regional Medical Center. By the time they got there the hospital was packed, filled with tanned soldiers in DCUs, awkwardly maneuvering their way down crowded hallways in wheelchairs and on crutches. The wounded soldiers gathered in twos and threes in the smoking and sitting areas, but the raucous banter that Kristina had come to expect from soldiers was ab-sent, replaced with vacant stares and silence. As she made her way down the hospital corridors, Kristina wondered what expe-riences those soldiers were revisiting behind their dead eyes and was stunned by the emptiness she saw in their gazes. The soldiers had been gone for such a short time, but already everything in their world had changed. Instead of the joyful reunions they had envisioned, these soldiers would be reunited with their loved ones here, in a hospital bed far from home. It shouldn't happen that way, she thought, as she observed an exhausted middle-aged couple asking a nurse for directions to their son's ward.

The two friends were stunned by what they had seen at the

hospital, and decided to find a way to put their feelings into words. They dedicated an open letter, titled "The True Heroes," to the troops and anyone else who cared to read it, hoping that it would in some small measure let the soldiers know how much they were missed and appreciated by everyone on the home front. Kristina wrote,

> *No matter what your stand regarding the war in Iraq or your political affiliation, you must realize the very real hardships and dangers these men and women in uniform are facing. My husband is currently deployed and when I talk to him on the phone he always says he is doing fine. Then, in his letters, he writes about the conditions they have to live in right now and I just wonder how he can say he is doing fine. Let me tell you, I would not be able to handle it.*
>
> *…I most definitely could not handle being separated from my kids for that long. It is not easy sometimes for us back here that are around the kids. We have to deal with their attitudes, their frustration about their Daddy not being here. Try to explain to a two-year-old little girl that her Daddy is in Iraq and won't be back for a year. You keep telling them that Daddy will be back soon, but it seems that they do not believe it anymore. You try to make it easier by showing them pictures and videos of their Daddy as often as you can, but sometimes you just have to turn it off because it hurts too much to even watch it.*
>
> *…It is not easy to sit down and write to your husband that his son, who he barely knows, just got his first two teeth and has the cutest little smile now. For us it is hard not to be able to share [these things] with our husbands.*
>
> *But how much harder must it be to be the man not being there to see those things, reading about how your kids are doing, but the letter is already weeks old by the time you finally receive it? How upsetting must it be to be separated from your children, not able to see them grow up, not knowing whether or not they will accept you when you get back?*
>
> *…When I think of my husband personally I think of him*

being home, doing what he always does. When I think of him being down there I don't just think of him; I think of his soldiers, his commanders, and a countless amount of other soldiers that are down there along with him.... In a way I feel connected to them all and I love them in a certain way, just because they ARE heroes, fighting with my husband, risking their lives for somebody else's freedom.

...Honestly, I never liked my husband's job. I don't like being separated from him, having to worry about his safety. But I DO know how much pride I feel when I tell people my husband is in Iraq.

That evening, Kristina printed out a copy of the letter and put it in an envelope addressed to Scott, then visited each of the children's bedrooms before heading to bed herself. Tyler was sleeping peacefully, but Marie's eyes opened when she heard her mother's approaching footsteps. "Mama?" she called out sleepily.

"I'm here, Marie," Kristina replied, stroking the little girl's back, which was draped in the only nightgown she had agreed to wear since her father left, one of Scott's well-worn brown Army t-shirts.

"I want my daddy," Marie said. "Where's my daddy?"

As she had every night for the past two months, Kristina patiently reminded her daughter about the big bus that had taken her father away to work, and once again, she told the lie that was the only word she could bear to tell her. "Soon," she said. "He'll be home soon."

ONE GLASS, NOT THREE

Teresa knew all too well that Danny was not coming home soon, and by July her resentment of that fact nearly consumed her. As Danny's scent gradually faded from his pillow, the calmness she had felt the morning after his departure had also vanished, giving way first to anger and then to piercing depression. Over and over her mind replayed the scene of their goodbye: Danny getting out of the car and starting to walk away without giving her the slightest indication that he felt bad about leaving.

Each time she revisited the scene she felt more betrayed. She was angry that Danny had left the way he had, angry that he had pushed her away when he should have been drawing her close, angry that she was in this rotten situation in the first place.

On a sweltering afternoon in early July, Teresa received her first letter from Danny. Sitting in her car parked in front of the community mailroom, she tore open the letter, skimming past reports of sandstorms and five-inch spiders, searching for words of affection. She didn't have to search long. Danny had written mainly to apologize for the way he had acted before he deployed. He explained that he hadn't known how to handle saying goodbye, and that pulling away from her had been the only way he had known how to get through the painful separation. He hadn't meant to shut her out, but he knew he had done just that, and he was sorry. He promised to make it up to her when he got back.

His apology fell on deaf ears. Teresa shoved the letter into her purse and screeched out of the parking lot, heading home at break-neck speed. All Danny's apology had done was prove to her that he had known what he was doing all along, and all she wanted to do now was forget about it. As soon as she got home she poured herself a glass of wine. When she finished the first glass she poured herself another one, then another, until the entire bottle was gone.

The next morning arrived in a blur. Teresa covered up her puffy eyes with extra eyeliner and mascara, hoping her co-workers at the Education Center wouldn't notice how tired she looked. Sorting through a pile of trendy new clothes she had bought the previous weekend and promptly tossed onto the bedroom floor, she chose her favorite new skirt and blouse, and then hair sprayed her short new haircut into place. Good enough, she thought as she examined her reflection.

On her way out the door, she paused for a moment as she walked past Danny's West Point diploma. At 24 by 18 inches, his United States Military Academy diploma dwarfed her standard-size diploma from UCLA. Bothered by the vast empty space underneath her own diploma, Teresa had filled the hole with the only thing she had on hand: two framed certificates she and Danny had received upon completion of a 30-minute beer appreciation seminar at Sea World. Appropriately ridiculous, she had decided when she put them up. She had been so proud of her college diploma when she got it but now, looking at it next to Danny's, it looked woefully inadequate. Pretty symbolic, she thought. Here I am, heading to a dead end job, filling out paper work in the testing center, while Danny's off doing exactly what he wants.

Carl Blackwell[1], a retired Air Force mechanic currently in a second career as an academic counselor at the Army Education Center, was the first to greet her as she walked into her second floor office in the testing center. "Hey Teresa!" he said warmly. "You look nice today. Do something different?"

"Hah. Hah," Teresa replied flatly, rolling her eyes. Sensing something was wrong, Carl followed her into her office and took a seat across from her desk. Teresa put on a cheery smile for a passing coworker's benefit, but as soon as the woman was out of eyesight Teresa's smile vanished. Carl was one of the few people at the Ed. Center she could be straight with, one of the few people in Baumholder, really, and there was no use pretending that everything was fine when he could look at her in a minute and tell she was mess. "Okay, let's hear it," Carl said, leaning back in his chair and crossing his fingers over the top of his cornrowed head. "What'd he do this time?"

Teresa motioned with her eyes for Carl to shut the door and reached instinctively for the box of tissues she had kept on her desk ever since Danny deployed. Her eyes brimming with tears, she told Carl about the letter. Danny had no right to think that one stupid letter was going to make everything okay, she said. Nothing was okay. Her attempts to get pregnant before Danny left had been fruitless. She had barely seen him in the months before he left, and now she wasn't going to see him at all for a whole year, assuming he even made it back. And he never called her! Everyone else she knew had heard from her husband several times by now, so where the hell was Danny?

Carl, who had fallen into the role of informal therapist for the many women at the Center whose husbands were deployed, waited until Teresa had finished her rant, placed one hand on her shoulder, and asked, "Do you think that part of the reason you're so mad at Danny might just be because you miss him?"

"No," Teresa said sharply. Carl raised his eyebrows. "Well, yes. Maybe," she admitted, "but...God, Carl. This sucks!"

"I know it does," Carl replied. "Have you written to him yet?"

Teresa shook her head adamantly. "No. That just makes it worse. I don't want him to know what happened to me three weeks ago; I want to be able to tell him what's happening right now! All a letter is going to do is remind me that I can't."

Teresa and Danny had been through years of long-distance dating during college, but they had never written letters; thanks to the Internet and recently relaxed rules at West Point, they had never had to. Every day they had communicated either by phone or email, which had made the miles between them seem much more tolerable. They had neither the phone nor email now. Phone connections in Danny's sector were hard to come by and the Internet access that commanders kept promising had yet to be set up. Teresa stubbornly refused to give in to a less efficient medium.

"Okay, Teresa," Carl said. "You're wrong, but okay. But I can tell you this: You love Danny. And he *does* love you, although I'm not sure why; you're such a pain in the neck sometimes." He waited for the corners of Teresa's mouth to betray a smile, and then finished his thought. "You'll get through this."

Their conversation was interrupted by a knock on the door. "I'll check in on you later, okay?" Carl said. Teresa nodded, dabbing away a stray tear from the corner of one eye.

"Hi!" she said cheerfully to the soldier who came limping into the room on crutches. "Welcome home!" And then, acknowledging his leg, she asked, "You going to be okay?"

"No big deal," the soldier answered, brushing his injury aside with a wave of his hand. "I just wanna get back down there."

"Yeah, that's what they all say," Teresa replied. "Okay, I just need to see some ID and I can get you started on your test."

A few weeks later, Teresa's parents flew out to Germany for a visit. Her mother was immediately concerned by Teresa's appearance. She was wearing much more make-up than usual, clearly intended to conceal dark circles under her eyes. And even though

Teresa had barely eaten all summer, she had gained weight on her new "liquid diet." Though Teresa was still barely over 100 pounds, her mother noticed the slight weight gain on her daughter's tiny frame, thinking that the weight wouldn't have been unattractive at all had she not appeared so malnourished.

While Teresa's physical appearance had caused concern, Teresa's mother found her daughter's choice of friends even more worrying. By Teresa's own admission, several of the new friendships she had formed over the summer were with women in unhappy marriages who, from Teresa's mother's point of view, seemed to be spending an inordinate amount of time out at local bars. Teresa's mother also noticed that her daughter, who she knew remained just as smitten with Danny as she had been the day she married him, never so much as mentioned his name in the presence of her friends except to complain.

"Mija," her mother said, using the Spanish term of endearment for a daughter, "I just want you to be careful. I don't think these new friends of yours are a good influence."

Teresa was indignant at what she saw as maternal meddling, and disregarded her mother's judgment as ill-informed and inappropriate. She was an adult—an independent, married woman—and she was certainly capable of choosing her own friends.

Later that day, still tense from their earlier conversation, Teresa and her mother and father stopped at restaurant for lunch. A waitress approached the table and asked for their drink order.

"I'd like a bottle of red wine," Teresa said.

"Three glasses?" the waitress asked.

"No, just one," Teresa replied stonily, and proceeded to drink the entire bottle while her parents looked on in dismay.

RUINED DREAMS

While Teresa sunk deeper into depression, Diane struggled with sorrows of a different kind. A loner by nature, the deployment had only increased her isolation. The only people she ever saw were her coworkers at her new job in the community mailroom and her two young sons, Brian, age 8, and Michael, age

3. She longed for friends in the community and had hoped to build closer relationships with her neighbors during the deployment. She had heard that the military communities in Europe tended of be closer than those back in the States, that people were cut off from their comfort zones and subsequently tended to bond together more than usual. It had been a grave disappointment when she found that, at least in her case, European military communities were no different from the ones at home. She had made a few attempts to be friendly and meet people when she first moved into her building, but had aborted the effort when her neighbors failed to reciprocate. It seemed she was going to have to face the deployment alone.

But one warm summer evening a few of her neighbors invited her to join them at the picnic table in front of their building. Kids played outside, taking advantage of the summer sun and relaxed curfew, and Diane sat with the adults, enjoying a rare moment of camaraderie. She stayed out until about 10:00 p.m., and as she climbed the three flights of stairs to her apartment she thought how nice it was to have some company for a change. She got the boys bathed and into bed, then checked the answering machine, hoping that she hadn't missed a call from Thomas. Sure enough, the first message was from him. He had access to a satellite phone that night, he said, and he needed to talk to her right away. The next message was also from Thomas, his voice becoming agitated. Where could she be at 9 p.m. on a weeknight? It was late; she should be home by now. He had called 22 times within half an hour, each call revealing an increasing level of panic.

By the time he finally reached her he was frantic. "Where have you been?" he demanded.

"Relax," she said, explaining her evening with the neighbors.

He had imagined horrible things, he told her. At first he thought that she might have been in a car accident, but then he started picturing other disturbing images: she was with another man; she was cheating on him. Diane promised him that there was no other man. She got lonely at times, she admitted, but she wasn't going out and looking for anything. Thomas sounded unconvinced. Cheating wives was the number one topic of conversation in the barracks downrange. According to the rumors, life back in Baumholder was a veritable orgy. Diane sighed. "Well, I guess you are just going to have to believe me," she told him.

Only then did Thomas disclose the real reason for his frantic calls. Something terrible had happened that day, and he wanted her to hear it from him first.

That morning Thomas had gone to Baghdad International Airport as part of a convoy. As the noncommissioned officer (NCO) in charge of a tank on the mission, he was ultimately responsible for the actions of his crew. Unfamiliar with the crew, which he had met for the first time that morning, and its training, Thomas assigned a young soldier to serve as gunner on the return trip, the same soldier who had been slated for that role during an earlier mission but who had been removed just before the convoy departed. Thomas helped the soldier into position and was climbing into the tank when he heard a loud explosion coming from the vehicle; the gunner had fired his weapon, nearly hitting a convoy of American soldiers with the round.

No one was injured, but the shots could easily have been deadly. The gunner claimed that the gun had misfired, but when the company commander investigated, repeated efforts to bring about an accidental firing proved that there was nothing wrong with the gun; the soldier had made a mistake. Only later was it discovered that the soldier had never received the mandatory training on the gun and was, therefore, not qualified to serve in that position. It was a fact that Thomas, as the sergeant in charge, was expected to have known. The punishment for the gunner (for the negligent discharge) and for Thomas (for failure to supervise) was likely to be severe.

Thomas told Diane that the company commander was making a decision about what his punishment would be, and he was worried that the chain of command was going to come down hard on him, possibly resulting in a demotion and loss of pay. Thomas had lost rank earlier in his career for various forms of misconduct and, he told Diane ruefully, losing rank again could end his career in the Army for good.

FALL

Skewered by his absences, she felt a side of her emerging that she knew wasn't particularly appealing. Where was her self-sufficiency, her self-respect? ...She envied those wives who seemed so plucky and contained, who gave their husbands a peck on the forehead and a pat on the cheek with a "Darlin', you just go and take good care of yourself." How do they do that? she wondered. What price did they pay, those wives who were left alone for weeks, months, years over the course of a marriage?

—The Long Gray Line *by Rick Atkinson*

CHAPTER SIX

"My question to Mr. Bush is, how many more of our sons do you need to [die before you] bring our children home?"
— *Fernando Suarez del Solar,*
member of the Bring Them Home Now campaign and father of
Marine Lance Cpl. Jesus Suarez, one of the first U.S. servicemen killed in Iraq,
reacting to President Bush's "bring 'em on" statement

"The number of U.S. service members who have died in Iraq since the end of the major phase of the war now surpasses the toll in the first phase of the conflict."
— *CNN, August 26, 2003*

DEATH COMES TO BAUMHOLDER

Staff Sergeant Kimmerly was looking forward to going home. He kept a photo of his wife and son in his wallet, and often pulled out the photo to reexamine their faces. It was his fourth month in Iraq and he was long overdue to return to Baumholder and transfer to a different unit based in the States; he was eager for the Army's stop move policy to be lifted so that he and his family could go on to their next assignment.

He had been in the Army for 12 years, and it was obvious to his fellow soldiers that he loved it. Having served tours in Bosnia and Kosovo, he was experienced and often served as a mentor to the young lieutenant leading his platoon who frequently sought out the veteran soldier's guidance.

Early on the morning of Sept. 15th 2003, 26 days before he was scheduled to return to Germany, Staff Sergeant Kimmerly geared up for patrol. The brutal heat of the Iraqi summer had begun to relent only slightly, and even in the relative coolness of the predawn hours he and the crew stewed under their helmets and body armor as they climbed into two ammo-carrying vehicles and set off on a routine patrol, heading down dusty, trash-strewn streets lined with sewage and goats. The large, unarmored, tracked vehicles were noisy and cumbersome, not designed for urban missions, and provided the soldiers inside little protection as they entered one of the more dangerous neighborhoods in the district. As the vehicles passed a dilapidated high-rise apartment building, each soldier heightened his alert level; the building had become a common hiding site for "bad guys," as the soldiers referred to their numerous enemies. Staff Sergeant Kimmerly and the soldiers with him trained their guns on the building, examining each passage for a sign of hidden danger.

Suddenly, seemingly out of nowhere, a violent explosion rocked the crew; an RPG (rocket propelled grenade) had slammed into the vehicle. There was little overall damage to the vehicle, but Staff Sergeant Kimmerly had taken a direct hit. His left arm hung limply from his body, nearly severed from the blast, and it was clear that he had suffered massive abdominal injuries. The driver sped away from the scene of the attack, delivering the injured soldier to the rally point. Army medics did what they could to sustain him, but by the time he was airlifted to a field hospital he had lost so much blood that there was little hope of survival. Upon word of the injuries, every soldier in the battalion with a matching blood type lined up to donate blood, but their efforts were futile; Staff Sergeant Kimmerly's internal injuries were too serious for the blood to clot. The members of his platoon hovered around the radio in silence, waiting for news of his condition and praying that by some miracle his wounds might not turn out to be as dire as they had seemed. Their prayers went unanswered.

At 8:05 a.m. Staff Sergeant Kimmerly was declared dead. He was the first soldier from Baumholder to die in combat.[1]

THE PHOTO STUDIO IS DOWN THE STREET
AND ON THE LEFT

"Did you hear about that soldier who got killed yesterday?" Tasha's beautician asked as she streaked chemicals onto her hair.

Tasha looked up from the magazine she had been flipping through. "What? No. Who? What unit?" Her thoughts flew immediately to Anthony, even though common sense told her that if it had been her husband who was killed, she wouldn't be finding out about it at the beauty salon.

"He was field artillery," the beautician answered. "I'm not sure what unit."

Tasha aimed her eyes heavenward and silently thanked God for having spared her husband. She had been waiting for this to happen—not this particular soldier, of course, but with soldiers dying in Iraq every day, it was only a matter of time before death came to Baumholder. Still, she found the news chilling. "Lord, lord," she said, shaking her head slowly from side to side. "Was he married?"

"Yeah. His wife's here in Baumholder and I think they have a kid, poor thing. There's gonna be a memorial service for him tomorrow, if you want to go."

Tasha wasn't sure at first. She had never met the widow; the soldier wasn't in Anthony's battalion. But the next morning she found herself inexplicably drawn to the service. As she walked down the sidewalk toward the large, white chapel, she warily eyed the soldiers in front of the entrance in their formal Class A uniforms, standing at parade rest. During a deployment, Class A uniforms, which under normal circumstances are benignly worn for official photographs and functions, take on a sinister connotation. Every spouse of a deployed soldier knows to prepare for the worst if a soldier in a starched, dark green suit jacket with medals pinned across the chest appears at the door.

Tasha turned away from the grave-looking soldiers and focused on making her way through the crowd of black-clad mourners to one of the back pews. Once everyone had been seated, an Army chaplain took the pulpit and offered a prayer in honor of the fallen soldier, speaking of his heroism and sacrifice. Tasha shook her head, thinking that this wasn't about heroism or sacrifice at all; it was about a wife who was never going to see her husband again, about a child who had just lost his father. Even though she didn't know the widow, she had never felt so sorry for anyone in her life, and prayed that she would never find herself in that woman's shoes.

In the Army ritual for a fallen soldier, the first sergeant from the soldier's unit stands in front of his company and calls out three or more names. The first names called are of soldiers who are present, each of whom responds, "Here, First Sergeant!" Then the name of the fallen soldier is called once, twice, and then a third time, for which there will never be a response.

The mission required that the company's first sergeant remain with the rest of his unit in Baghdad, so a high-ranking enlisted soldier left behind with the rear detachment carried out his grim duty instead. After the chaplain had finished speaking, the soldier stood to read roll call and Tasha braced herself for the unbearable silence that was about to come.

His body held straight in a rigid military pose, the soldier called out,

"Staff Sergeant Kimmerly!"
No response.

"Staff Sergeant Kevin Kimmerly!"
No response.

And finally, "Staff Sergeant Kevin Christopher Kimmerly!"

But for a few stifled sobs, the chapel was silent. Then, a lone bugler began to play "Taps," and the sobs grew louder.

Tasha dabbed the tears away from her eyes, fighting to regain her composure. No matter how many times she heard roll call, its impact never diminished. As soon as they got to the fallen soldier's name, never to be answered, it always broke her up. Everyone was crying. Women, soldiers, everyone. Tasha couldn't watch as the widow and her young son walked down the center aisle and out of the chapel, her mind filled with a single thought: That could have been any one of us, she thought. Any one of us.

The next morning Tasha was awoken by two quick knocks on her bedroom door.

"Bye, Mom!" Keisha yelled. "I'm goin' to school."

"Oh no you don't!" Tasha called out sleepily. "You aren't going anywhere until I get a look at what you're wearing!"

Keisha popped her head into her mother's darkened bedroom, letting out an exaggerated sigh of exasperation.

"Come closer," Tasha said. Keisha, who was dressed conservatively in jeans and an oversized t-shirt, reluctantly succumbed to the examination. "Okay," Tasha said. "Now you can go. Be good."

"I will, Mom," Keisha called out as she exited the apartment. Tasha knew she didn't have much to worry about with her precocious 15-year-old daughter. The girl was nearly a straight-A student and was already making plans for college but still, Tasha kept a vigilant watch over her only child to make sure she didn't step out of line.

Tasha slid back under the covers, clutching her pillow tightly. Unable to face the hours alone in the apartment, she shut her eyes and tried to return to sleep, hoping it would shield her from the interminable day ahead. Her days weren't always like this. On her better days, she would see Keisha off to school, run a few errands, scour the apartment that she habitually kept as clean as a surgical ward, and look through her wedding album for what seemed like the 150 millionth time, still marveling at what a handsome man she had married, what a good man.

Tasha had met Anthony only a few years earlier, when she was in her late thirties and still serving in the Army at Fort Hood, Texas. They had met before through the local Masonic organization, but Tasha had never given him much thought. Since becoming pregnant with Keisha, the result of a dead-end relationship, she had been leery of men. She'd had only two relationships since becoming a mother, one of which ended in heartbreak, and that was not the kind of situation Tasha wanted her daughter to witness again. But one night at a party a friend commented that the handsome, broad-shouldered soldier several years Tasha's junior was staring at her and, apparently, had told several people that he was interested. It's high school all over again, Tasha had thought at the time, but when he asked her out later that night, she accepted.

It was hardly an ideal time to start a romantic relationship. The very next day after their first date, Tasha went into the hospital for a hysterectomy. When she opened her eyes in the recovery room, drugged up and groggy, she was perplexed to find Anthony sitting beside her bed. She faded in and out of sleep, and each time she opened her eyes he was the first person she saw. Anthony nursed her back to health, and before her recovery was complete she knew she was falling in love.

Keisha, however, was not so easily convinced. As the only child of a single military mother, Keisha had formed an exceptionally strong bond with her mom. It had always been the two of them against the world, a status that seemed imperiled by the sudden arrival of a potential stepfather. Making matters worse, Keisha remembered well the pain her mother's previous relationship had caused and saw it as her duty to drive off the newcomer before he abandoned them of his own free will. She had nothing against Anthony in particular, but she was not going to let any man intrude on their household without a fight.

As time passed, Keisha's opposition to her mother's romance lessened, but Tasha worried about the effect Anthony's presence was having on her own relationship with her daughter. They had always been close, but as the three of them searched for a new way to be a family, Keisha seemed to be pulling away from her. For Tasha, Keisha's sudden remoteness was the only damper on what was otherwise the most deliriously happy period of her life. Long after she had given up on love, it had finally found her.

Baumholder was their first duty station as a family and, having completed the 20-year commitment for earning a full military pension, Tasha decided to retire. Between Anthony's paycheck and her pension, they had more than enough money to meet their needs. More importantly, she feared that the post-9/11 Army would require simultaneous deployments, leaving Keisha with no one to care for her. For the first time in her life, Tasha became a stay-at-home mom. Her life revolved around three things: her husband, her daughter, and the church, and she needed all three in order to feel whole.

Driven out of bed by hunger, Tasha padded across the carpeted floor to the large television screen that dominated the living room, turned on CNN, and started toward the kitchen. Scenes of soldiers racing to the scene of a recent explosion filled the living room, causing Tasha to forget her hunger and sit down instead on a leather La-Z-Boy recliner placed directly opposite the television screen.

Just then the phone rang. Tasha dashed to the phone, torn between the conflicting emotions of excitement and dread. It could be Anthony, calling at last. Anthony belonged to one of the unfortunate companies that had been allotted a base with few creature comforts: no running water, no generators to run the air conditioners, few phones, and no Internet access. Tasha knew that he often waited in line two hours and more to call her, and she routinely waited by the phone for hours on end, determined never to miss a call. On the other hand, it could be someone calling to tell her that something terrible had happened. Wives had been told that if their husbands were killed, they would be informed within 12 hours, 24 if they were injured. And so, whenever CNN broadcast news of yet another attack against U.S. forces, the countdown began.

As it turned out, the phone call was neither, just a friend from the FRG calling to remind her about a meeting scheduled for later that week. Tasha leaned back against a kitchen cabinet and waited for her heart to stop racing. What a crazy way to live, she thought, nearly having a heart attack every time the phone rang. The only thing worse was seeing the approach of headlights, hearing two car doors slam, and then waiting for a knock on the door. She imagined the scene at Staff Sergeant Kimmerly's apartment the night the soldiers in Class A uniforms had come for the unsuspecting widow, and knew just what she would do if anyone came knocking on her door: "If anyone comes to my door in a Class A uniform," she had told a friend from church, "I am going to tell 'em that the photo studio is down the street on the left. Get away from my house!"

SOMETHING GOOD

Unlike Tasha, who lived just one floor below her in the same stairwell, Jena refused to let herself even think about the possibility of that dreaded knock on the door. Instead, she focused her attention on a lengthy to-do list she had written out shortly after Adam left. The list included fun tasks such as taking trips to neighboring countries with her girlfriends and organizing her photo collection into scrapbooks, as well as other goals like straightening up their disorganized storage compartment, losing a few excess pounds, and becoming even more active in her family readiness group.

Increasing her involvement in her company's FRG was Jena's first project. Even though soldiers from Baumholder were already in Iraq, new families were arriving on post every week and she knew they would need help getting settled in as their husbands in-processed and immediately headed off to join their units. Jena taught classes designed to help new Army spouses learn the many acronyms and regulations required for comprehending life in the Army, volunteered to give newcomers rides to the commissary and health clinic, cooked for mothers with new babies, and started an adopt-a-soldier program to boost morale among the single soldiers downrange. But the project she was most proud of was a campaign to get celebrities to send messages of support to the troops. The response was overwhelming and she soon had more letters and celebrity paraphernalia than she knew what to do with.

Surveying the flood of responses, she thought how glad she was to be able to be a part of the military at a time like this. "Not only have I gained things from this [military] life," she told a friend, "but I have seen so much good in humanity." Jena was deeply touched by the messages of support that were sent to her from friends and strangers alike, messages that reinforced her belief that she and Adam were a part of something bigger than them- selves, something good.

Wanting to be a part of something good was one the reasons Jena had been attracted to Adam in the first place. Like many other military couples, Jena and Adam began dating in high school. Adam, two years her senior, was the youth leader for a local charity, and one evening at a meeting he caught Jena's eye. She was impressed with the confidence he exuded as he spoke, and she was even more intrigued by his dedication to helping people, a commitment she shared.

She began flirting with him every way she could think of—stealing his baseball hat, teasing him playfully, making up excuses to see him—but Adam, who Jena says is "utterly naïve when it comes to women flirting with him," didn't get the hint. It was his mother who finally clued him in two months later that Jena seemed to have a crush on him. He asked her out on a date, and within a month they were discussing marriage.

Three years later they were married, embarking on a period Jena refers to as a typical suburban dream life, complete with their own home, a big yard, a dog, and an SUV. Jena found a rewarding job working for the Alabama Supreme Court while Adam made plans to enter the Army's Officer Candidate School as soon as he completed his bachelor's degree in civil engineering. He had two semesters to go when the 9/11 attacks changed his plans.

On the morning of September 11th 2001, Jena and Adam were both home in bed, sick with the flu. They were awoken by a phone call from Jena's mother, calling to ask if they had seen the news. They turned on the television set just in time to watch in horror as a second plane crashed into the World Trade Center. By the end of the day, with Jena's complete support, Adam had decided to enlist in the Army. Two years later he was in Iraq and Jena was building a new life for herself, alone, in Baumholder.

Coming from a small Southern town in which civic duties were taken seriously, getting involved in the community seemed like the most natural thing in the world to Jena, not to mention the fact that staying busy and helping people was the best way she had found to keep her mind off of her own worries. She knew people who sat at home all day, wishing they could fast forward the year away, and she didn't know how they got through it.

But even Jena, with her can-do attitude and positive outlook, wasn't immune to fears for Adam's safety. She, too, kept her television set tuned to CNN whenever she was home, and the images she saw were sometimes more than she could wish away. One afternoon, just as she was putting the finishing touches on a casserole she had made to share with a friend, news of an explosion in Baghdad caught her attention. There were casualties, but the reporter didn't know how many, nor did he give any precise information about where the attack had occurred. It was impossible to know if Adam had been close by, and Jena scolded herself for even considering the possibility that he might have been. Pull it together, she admonished herself. There's no reason to fall apart. But despite her efforts, she soon found her eyes filling with tears. She picked up the phone and dialed her mother's number.

"Hi Mom," she said in a wavering voice when her mother answered. "No, everything's fine." She paused and exhaled deeply. "I'm just having a crappy day and need you to put me back together again."

Jena listened as her mother reminded her that Adam was a good soldier, well-trained and smart, and that God was watching over him. Jena believed that, she really did, but some days tested her faith. It was one thing to have faith that God would protect Adam when all she had to worry about was him getting home safely from his daily commute, she thought. Keeping that faith when people were shooting at him required a whole new level of conviction.

THE BUST

Diane, too, felt her faith being tested, not in God, but the Army. Several weeks after the incident on the tank, Thomas called Diane to tell her that his chain of command had decided his punishment for his role in the misfire. Just as he had feared, Thomas's punishment was severe. He was issued a field grade Article 15[2], and with it he was docked pay, assigned 45 days of extra duty, and demoted one rank, dropping from a sergeant, an E-5, to a specialist, an E-4. Beyond the humiliation and the return to a lower pay grade, the bust meant that the soldiers who had once been Thomas's subordinates were now his peers; any authority he once had in his platoon was gone.

Reaching for a picture frame she kept on a table behind the couch, Diane examined the two side-by-side photos, one of her father-in-law and the other of her husband, both in their Class A uniforms. Thomas looked so proud in that uniform, so sure of himself. Even though he chafed under the authority of his platoon sergeants and young officers, being a soldier was actually the only thing Thomas had ever wanted to do. His father had fought in Korea, and Thomas's greatest desire was to follow in his father's footsteps. He had hoped to one day rise to the rank of sergeant major but that, Diane thought bitterly, was before recent events in Iraq dashed that hope forever.

Diane knew that Thomas was not the easiest person to get along with, and it was not a stretch to assume that he had stepped on so many toes in his chain of command that the leadership had been looking for a reason to bust him, but she still saw the penalty as grossly unfair. The soldier who had fired the weapon had received a demotion, a punishment that, due to his brief time in the Army, would have little effect on his overall military career. That soldier would be allowed to move on to his next duty station and could pretend the incident never happened, but Thomas's military career was probably over. Army regulations prohibited any soldier who had not risen to the rank of E-5 or above after ten years of service from reenlisting. It was unlikely that Thomas would be able to earn back sufficient rank in his short window of time.

Getting out of the military was a scary prospect for Diane, who had always thought of herself as a gypsy. Having grown up in a military family and joined the Coast Guard straight out of high school, she had never lived anywhere longer than three years, and that suited her just fine. In fact, friends back home often teased her that she should have married a Marine so she could have moved every one to two years instead of every three to four. More importantly, she knew from experience that without the Army's rigid structure and enforced professional commitment, Thomas's ability to hold down a steady job was uncertain. They had two sons to support now, and she had no desire to return to the financial instability that had plagued their early years of marriage.

Only a few months after their marriage, Thomas, fed up with constant clashes with his chain of command, had decided to leave the Army. He was sick of the Army and its inflexible hierarchy, sick of platoon sergeants and know-it-all, college-boy lieutenants breathing down his neck, and he was sure he could find something better in the civilian world. What followed was a string of dead-end jobs, most of which lasted no more than a few months. He worked at a bakery, sold vacuum cleaners and perfume door to door, and worked construction, but none of the jobs lasted. As soon as he got tired of a job, he quit. Meanwhile, Diane took whatever menial job she could find—once working at a zoo cleaning bathrooms and the massive piles of excrement left by the animals—anything to scrape together enough money to cover their bills. Every few months Thomas decided to move, promising that the new location would bring job security and a better life, but each move only brought more of the same.

They were on their third move in half as many years when Diane discovered that she was pregnant. She told Thomas that, for the sake of both their unborn child and their marriage, he simply had to reenlist. They needed a reliable income, and reenlisting in the Army seemed like the only way Thomas was going to get and keep a steady paycheck. It was the only place he had ever been consistent because, unlike his other jobs, the Army simply wouldn't let him quit.

Thomas reenlisted, and although the soldier's salary didn't make them rich, it was dependable. Thomas continued to fight with his chain of command, picking fights and taking noble but ultimately foolish stands on behalf of his subordinates that often led to punishment and demotion, but at least the job was stable. No matter how much he wanted to quit at times, he had to stay until his enlistment contract was up. Now, chances were good that Thomas would have to leave the Army within a year of his return from Iraq, and Diane hoped that if that turned out to be the case, this time things would be different. She hoped that in the past few years Thomas might have matured enough to keep a steady job without the Army forcing him to stay.

CHAPTER SEVEN

With extended deployments and increasingly deadly attacks by Iraqi guerrillas, Defense Department officials are scrambling to combat a broader downturn in retention and recruitment that they fear is on the horizon.
—The Boston Globe[1]

GEORGE NEED NOT COME SEE ME

On a blustery early fall evening, Tasha, dressed casually in a baggy t-shirt and khaki pants, walked into the enormous ecumenical church on Ramstein Air Base. The church was home to congregations of a wide variety of faiths—Episcopal, Catholic, Baptist—but tonight it was reserved for the teen gospel choir, a boisterous group of 20 or so African-American and mixed-race teens from several nearby U.S. Army and Air Force bases.

Tasha had become the choir director by default. The previous director had left soon after Tasha and Anthony moved to Baumholder, and though the church had searched for a replacement for weeks, no one had come forward. It looked as though they might have to cancel teen choir that year until, one afternoon while driving home from church, Tasha and Anthony turned to one another with the same idea: They could do it together. Tasha had previous experience leading a choir, and although Anthony had never done it before, he had always loved music and dreamed of leading a high school marching band once he retired from the Army. They took over immediately, and when Anthony deployed to Iraq, Tasha continued the work on her own with Keisha's enthusiastic participation.

As the teens ambled into the church, many of the girls still in

gym clothes from basketball practice, Tasha greeted them all with
playful teasing and an occasional hug, scolding the latecomers
with a sternness that only thinly veiled the depth of her fondness
for these young people.

"You're late!" she shouted to two girls who came strolling in
several minutes past the scheduled start of choir practice. "You're
gonna owe me essays."

"Aww, Ms. Washington," pleaded one girl. "Don't be like that.
Our ride was late. It wasn't our fault."

"I don't take excuses," Tasha replied. "And I make the rules,
not you. I want 400 words on tardiness. And *is* and *the* don't count!"

The girls groaned, but as they shuffled toward the piano to
join their peers they agreed to have the essays for her the following week.

Many of the choir members attended different high schools
and did not see one another during the day, so when they met
again for the first time that week, the result was a cacophony of
laughter and all the week's news. Tasha had to shout to get their
attention over the din. Eventually the teenagers settled down and
listened as the pianist introduced their various parts. Although
Tasha was more comfortable singing alto, she jumped back and
forth between the alto and soprano sections, keeping everyone
on key and breaking up side conversations. Often the teens seemed
far more interested in talking than singing, and Tasha harangued
them to stay on task. "I know you can do it," she encouraged a girl
who had just delivered her solo in a barely audible whisper. "I
hear you yakking all the time. Sing!"

Tasha drove them on relentlessly, demanding the performance
she knew they could deliver. They sang,

> *God is watching*
> *God is watching*
> *God is watching even now*
> *Though we don't know just where or how*
> *God is watching even now*

An hour later, at the end of practice, the group gathered

together in a circle, their hands linked in prayer.

"Does anyone have a special prayer they would like to mention?" Tasha asked.

One boy stepped forward, nodding in the direction of a female choir member. "I do. Tish's back has been causing her some serious pain. I'd like to ask God to help her recover soon."

"We'll do that," Tasha said. "Anyone else?"

"I have something to say," a gangly, soft-spoken girl who had entered choir practice wiping tears from her eyes chimed in. In a shaky, uncertain voice she said, "Most of you know that me and my mom have been havin' a lot of problems lately. We're gonna need all the prayers we can get."

Tasha nodded solemnly. "We should say a prayer for all family relationships. And please," she said after a pause, "remember the soldiers fighting in Iraq." The girl to Tasha's right squeezed her hand and mouthed the words, "He okay?"

Tasha smiled back, whispering, "So far."

The teens bowed their heads as the choir president, a boy who had quickly become Keisha's closest friend and confidant, led the group in prayer. As the teens gathered their backpacks and prepared to leave, Tasha pulled one of the girls aside. "How'd you do on that test last week?"

"I got a B," the girl responded proudly. "That's the best grade I ever got in algebra."

"I'm so proud of you!" Tasha exclaimed, wrapping the girl up in a warm hug. "Looks like the two of us have a date for ice cream coming up. Should I keep you on the call list?"

"Yes, Ma'am," the girl replied. "Having you on my case keeps me from slackin' off."

Tasha had several choir members on her "call list." Whenever their grades started to slip, she would begin her nightly phone calls, making sure the kids had done their homework and studied for upcoming exams. And when their grades improved, she also made sure there was a celebration. Since starting the list, several choir members had asked to be added, including one normally diligent student who claimed that he was suddenly having trouble in school. Tasha had begun calling him every evening, but it soon became apparent that the boy was not having problems in school at all. His grades were fine; his problems were at home. His parents were neglectful and totally disinterested in his progress, academic and otherwise, so he had sought out the support he craved from Tasha instead. Even though she knew he didn't need her help with his study habits, Tasha continued to call him nightly.

She looked on with satisfaction as the teens shouted goodbyes and hustled out the door. This, Tasha knew, was where she was at her best. The teens made her feel good. When she was down, they picked up on it and lifted her up. When she was doing okay, they made her feel even better. They were good kids, she thought, and a real blessing during this awful time. Twice a week, at Monday night choir practice and Sunday church, she felt almost happy. For those few hours each week, taking part in something that had been such an important part of the life she and Anthony shared and remembering that it was something they would, God willing, share once again, she felt a connection to her husband that was lost to her during the rest of the week. She only wished she knew when the long wait would be over.

Even now, months into the deployment, commanders remained frustratingly elusive about the division's return date: maybe April, maybe May, maybe even later than that. Despite President Bush's now infamous claim of "mission accomplished" back in May, the situation in Iraq had only became more savage as the Iraqi insurgents gained accuracy through practice. "It's like trying to salvage a burnt up Thanksgiving dinner," Tasha said of what she viewed as an increasingly futile occupation. "You can try all you like, but it can't be done."

The one thing she knew for certain was that nothing Anthony was doing in Iraq was worth dying for, and she had little patience for the President's televised condolences to the family members of soldiers killed in action. His daughters weren't the ones putting their lives on the line. Neither had he. "If I lose my husband," Tasha commented bitterly, "George [Bush] need not come see me."

NUMB

Kristina felt equally disillusioned, but the target of her wrath was not the Bush administration but the life she had chosen when she decided to get married at age 19. She was only 22 years old. She was supposed to be out having fun with her friends, going clubbing, staying out late, being irresponsible, but instead she was stuck at home seven days a week taking care of two kids and waiting for a phone call that never came.

Enough was enough. Kristina grabbed the phone hastily and dialed the number on the top of her FRG contact information phone list.

"Hello?" a woman's voice asked. Alison[2], who was the wife of Scott's new company commander, had taken over leadership of the FRG when her husband assumed command several months earlier. Kristina didn't know Alison well, and certainly didn't consider her a friend, but she wanted to know why she had heard from Scott so infrequently. It had been seven weeks since his last phone call. Alison was the only person she could think of who might have some answers.

"Hi," Kristina said tentatively. "It's Kristina. I'm sorry to bother you, but I haven't heard from my husband in a really long time and I…well…I was just wondering if you might know something. I don't know. Maybe he's off on some mission and away from the rest of the group, or something?"

Alison didn't know about any secondary missions, but she said she would ask her husband about it the next time he called.

"Thanks. I'd appreciate that," Kristina said in a faltering voice.

"Kristina, are you okay?" Alison asked.

"Not really," Kristina admitted. "I'm sick of this! It's pretty frustrating, you know? I have no idea where he is or what he's doing, and it's not like I can pick up the phone and call him."

Scott called a few days later, his voice betraying both concern and more than a little irritation. "My commander just called me in to tell me that I had better call home," Scott said soon after Kristina answered the phone. "He said you're really depressed or something. What's going on?"

Kristina was aghast. It had never occurred to her that Alison would divulge the contents of what she had assumed was a private conversation, much less that the message Scott would receive was that he had to call home because his wife was a basket case.

"Look, I'm not depressed," she said defensively. "I just told Alison that I was frustrated to not have heard from you for so long, okay? I think that is normal."

As a result of the commander's intervention, Scott started calling more regularly, though still far less frequently than Kristina would have liked. Even when he did call, their talks were unsatisfying; the phone calls were brief and often the connection was so bad that it was possible to relay only the most basic information: *I'm fine. The kids are fine. Marie had a cold but she is okay now. Tyler just got another tooth.* There was rarely any time to discuss anything personal, and often Kristina was so exasperated by the static and frequent disconnections that it didn't even seem worth the effort to try.

In the first months of the deployment Kristina had thought that the only way to get through it was to distance herself emotionally from her husband, and although she still saw some wisdom in that plan, she was disconcerted by how quickly it had happened. She hadn't wanted to believe she could feel so cut off from him so soon, that after less than half a year apart she could feel like she didn't even have a husband anymore.

Each week brought an increasing level of numbness until one day, when Scott asked her if she even missed him anymore, her honest answer was no, she didn't. So many months had passed since she had seen him, and they had shared so little in that time, that her life was starting to feel more normal without him in it. She didn't want to feel that way, and wondered if the pain of missing him would be better than the deadness inside her now, but with him still so far away and so many more months of separation ahead, she didn't know how to strengthen their ever-more tenuous bond. The pride she had once felt about being married to a soldier fighting in Iraq was still there, but added to it was the realization that if Scott stayed in the Army much longer, it might be at the expense of their marriage.

GOLD

Even Teresa, who had always been supportive of Danny's military career and had vowed never to become one of those military wives who gives her husband an ultimatum—the Army or me— was starting to consider the possibility of a life outside the Army. It had sneaked up on her little by little until, one evening during a phone call with Danny, she had nearly uttered the words she had promised never to speak.

"You need to relax and stop worrying about me so much," Danny had said over a crackly phone connection. "I'm fine. Really."

Listening to the sounds of mortar rounds and small arms fire reverberating in the background, Teresa found herself desperately wanting to shout, "Get out of the Army! Then I'll relax."

She often thought back to 9/11 and the shocking sight of college students in Cairo celebrating the collapse of the World Trade Center. She was dismayed now to see similar images on the nightly news of young Middle Eastern men celebrating American deaths. Listening to the politicians equivocate about the real reasons behind the war made her furious, and the news reports of attacks in Iraq never ceased to terrify her. She couldn't help thinking that the longer soldiers like Danny were over there, the greater the chance that they would never make it back at all. She had long ago abandoned hope of Danny coming home by Christmas; now all she wanted was for him to come home, period.

Teresa's worries about Danny's physical safety were matched only by her fears of what a year in a war zone would do to his mental state and, subsequently, their relationship. The daughter of a Vietnam veteran, Teresa knew all too well that the experiences of war could leave a permanent emotional scar on an entire family. Her father never talked to her about his military service, but it was clear that he had not left the pain of that war behind him. Lately, Teresa found herself haunted by a memory more than 20 years old. She and her father were watching television when an advertisement came on for a Time Life books series on the Vietnam War. Watching the ad, her father began to cry. She wanted to console him, but her mother instructed her to leave him alone and let him deal with it, which is what she did. It is what everyone in the family did, throughout years of her father's emotional distance from the family that Teresa felt certain were at least partially attributable to her father's experiences in Vietnam.

And so, as the months passed, Teresa carefully monitored Danny's tone in his calls and emails, trying to reassure herself that he was still the same laid back guy she had fallen in love with back in high school; that the connection they shared hadn't disappeared with the months of separation. He seemed fine for the most part, though a recent telephone conversation had made her nervous.

In the early fall Danny had been sent to the port in Kuwait to oversee the return of excess equipment to Baumholder. When he got there, he later told her, he was instructed to remove his gun; there was no need to wear it in Kuwait. But he had become so accustomed to keeping his gun with him 24-hours a day that being without it left him feeling naked. Teresa, who had rarely seen her husband armed, couldn't reconcile the image of the playful, lighthearted man she knew with the kind of person who would feel naked without a lethal weapon strapped to his back.

Not wanting to make an issue of it, she masked her discomfort with humor, and asked as lightly as she could, "So am I going to have to get you a toy gun to take with you to the commissary when you get back?" Then, hoping to get away from the uncomfortable subject, she said, "It's starting to get cold here. Pretty soon it will be time to take out my witch shoes." The 'witch shoes' were a pair of stylish, high-heeled boots her mother had given her the previous year for Christmas. Danny had teased her about them all winter, commenting that, with their long, pointy toes and tiny little heels, they looked like something a witch would wear. He warned that he could find her tracks in the snow everywhere she went because no one else wore such silly shoes in the middle of winter. The boots had become a running joke, and Teresa was sure Danny would catch the reference.

"What are witch shoes?" Danny asked without the slightest sign of comprehension.

Teresa couldn't believe he didn't remember. Granted, it was an insignificant, stupid thing to get upset about, but if he had forgotten about the witch shoes, then what else about their life together had he forgotten? "What do you mean you don't remember?" she asked, trying unsuccessfully to hide her disappointment.

Danny took a few seconds to answer, and then said, "I can't remember a lot of things, Teresa."

Only a short time earlier, Teresa's response to such a phone call would have been to automatically reach for a bottle, but in the past few weeks she had gradually begun to pull herself out of her debilitating depression. Increased communication with Danny and the reprieve from worry during his stay in Kuwait had helped stop her rapid downward spiral, but perhaps even more important was the return of her local support network to Baumholder. During her self-destructive summer months, Teresa had realized how caustic her behavior was, but had lacked the willpower and the peer support to change course. In early September, help had arrived.

Several officers' wives from her battalion had spent the summer visiting relatives back in the States. Teresa had been one of the few who had remained in Baumholder, causing her to link up with women she could now admit were not ideal choices as friends. As old friends and acquaintances from the battalion returned to Baumholder, many were shocked to see the state Teresa was in. Her bubbly, mischievous personality seemed to have been overcome by bitterness, and they worried about the amount she was drinking. Having a few of their favorite apple martinis on girls' night was one thing, drinking alone was another.

Teresa's friends rallied around her, helping her to start a work out regime, scheduling evening walks, and getting together on weekends to cook dinner and watch new episodes of TV's popular dating show, *The Bachelor*. They started a weekly tradition called Buddy Night, an informal gathering that functioned as half support group, half sorority meeting for the officers' and senior NCOs' wives in the battalion. They gathered every Friday night to eat, drink, tell stories, and laugh or cry, depending on how the week had gone. Slowly, Teresa began to feel and act like herself again. She severed her ties with the crowd she had associated with over the summer—unhappy people who had dragged her down with them, she now realized. She curtailed her drinking to a moderate amount on social occasions, started going to the gym regularly, and threw herself into the master's degree program in human relations she had started shortly before Danny deployed.

That fall two women from the group, Heather, a vivacious, cherubic-looking lieutenant's wife with wisps of blonde hair framing her round face, and Jennifer, a tall, statuesque captain's wife with olive skin and a cascade of brown curls, invited Teresa to join them on a weekend excursion to Euro Disney. Teresa didn't know either woman well beyond reputation. Heather was known in the battalion for her ability to crack up just about anyone, while Jennifer was widely respected as Heather's calmer, more reserved other half. Teresa hadn't known quite what to make of the pair, but by the time they got to the theme park she knew she had, in her words, "struck gold." Linking arms and giggling like schoolgirls as they raced from ride to ride, the three young women found that they had a tremendous amount in common. They liked the same TV shows—they all admitted a slightly embarrassing addiction to *Buffy the Vampire Slayer*. They shared the same offbeat sense of humor, held similar moral beliefs, and most of all, they all deeply loved their husbands.

For the first time in months, Teresa felt free to talk about Danny as much as she wanted. With Heather and Jennifer, she could share the touching or humorous comments Danny made in a phone call or email without worrying that they would think she was bragging or showing off. If she missed him, she could tell them, and when she got angry because weeks had passed without a phone call, she could tell them that, too. Whenever she vented her frustrations about a lag in communication either Heather or Jennifer would cheer her up by saying, "Girl, you're just mad because you miss him and he's gone. You have to remember he's in Iraq. He's doing the best he can and he loves you."

From that weekend on, Teresa, Heather, and Jennifer were inseparable. At least once a week the three friends met at Portifino's, an inexpensive but surprisingly good Italian restaurant in downtown Baumholder. They planned trips to antique markets in Poland and Belgium, flying down the autobahn at 120 miles an hour in Teresa's brand new BMW as they sang along to the Greatest Hits of the '80s at the top of their lungs. They spent hours shopping at a nearby outlet mall. Heather and Teresa went for trendier looks while Jennifer veered toward classier, more timeless pieces. In short, they became each other's lifeline, and after only a few weeks of friendship, Teresa could not begin to imagine getting through the rest of the deployment without them.

CHAPTER EIGHT

...the Pentagon announced the approval of a 15-day rest and recuperation program for soldiers serving 12-month combat tours. "This is the first time an R&R leave program has been provided in a combat theater for all forces on 12-month orders since Vietnam," said Maj. Pete Mitchell, spokesman for the U.S. Central Command.
—Stars and Stripes[1]

REST AND RECUPERATION

On September 26, 2003 CBS News reported, "A mortar blast tore through a market north of Baghdad, killing nine civilians, and a U.S. soldier was killed in an ambush in the north of the country as the American-led coalition struggles to maintain order five months after the ouster of Saddam Hussein." This latest attack raised the combat death toll to 86 since President Bush declared an end to major combat on May 1st, with no end in sight to the ongoing violence.

That same day CBS News also reported a more uplifting story: A planeload of soldiers taking part in the first rest and recuperation leave program (R&R) since Vietnam were on their way home. Two hundred and seventy troops had flown out of the region the day before, on their way to home bases in Germany and the United States. They would have 15 days to relax, spend time with friends and family, and enjoy the comforts of home before returning to the occupation. According to U.S. Central Command, the leave program, which was available to service members who had been "in theater" more than three months and were scheduled to serve a one-year tour, was designed to give service members "the opportunity to get away from the stresses associated with their missions and to focus on family and friends when they return home."

Back in Baumholder, rumors had spread through post about a possible R&R long before the official announcement was made; several spouses even claimed to know the exact date of their husbands' return, despite repeated statements from FRG and rear detachment leaders that no R&R rotation schedule had yet been determined. The reaction to the announcement was one of cautious excitement and some apprehension. Most spouses eagerly anticipated the long-awaited, albeit temporary reunion, while others greeted the news with skepticism, concerned that the brief interruption of established routines might do soldiers and their families more harm than good.

No more than 10 percent of the force in Iraq could be away from the unit simultaneously, which meant that not everyone would be coming home. According to the U.S. Central Command's official R&R website, "Although many service members are eligible for R&R leave, operational requirements within theater and the unit redeployment schedule will preclude many from participating in the R&R program." Commanders on the ground estimated that approximately 50 to 60 percent of the soldiers from Baumholder would be granted leave.[2]

With many soldiers likely to be denied the opportunity to come home, disappointment was inevitable. Some wives could not bear to think of having to watch some other woman reunited with her husband, strolling hand and hand through the video store or sitting together over a pizza, while they would have to endure the long and lonely remaining months of the deployment without reprieve. Furthermore, many feared that even if their husbands did come home, the pain of saying goodbye again might be too much to bear. They worried that, as Beth had already discovered when Doug returned to Iraq, it would be much harder to watch their husbands leave the second time around.

While some were afraid to get their hopes up for a visit that might never come to pass or a goodbye that would yield more heartache than the reunion would salve, others were apprehensive about the visit itself. Several Baumholder marriages, most of them less than a year old, had already collapsed under the strain of deployment. In the early fall, as soldiers once again appeared on post, most on their way to or coming from Iraq, the downtown clubs had been filled with single soldiers preying on lonely wives. Tales of infidelity spread rampantly between Baumholder and Iraq, and it seemed that everyone had a story (generally founded on nothing more substantial than idle gossip) about a cheating wife in her stairwell.[3] Rumor had it that some of the returned soldiers were even taking the new photo-capable cell phones out to clubs in order to catch unfaithful spouses in the act, sending the digital evidence back to suspicious buddies back in Iraq.

In one case, a newlywed came to see Captain Bromenshenkel shortly after hearing about the R&R program, asking him to prevent her husband from coming home. Her marriage had crumbled during the first few months of her husband's absence. By October she had already found a new boyfriend and feared that her husband might react violently when he found out that she planned to end their marriage. Captain Bromenshenkel agreed to find a room in the barracks for the woman's husband in order to provide her with some measure of protection and offered to call in a chaplain to assist in the unhappy reunion, but told the woman that if her husband got one of the coveted slots for R&R, he was not going to stop him from coming home.

This, however, was an extreme case. Most spouses were more typical of Diane, who had remained faithful to her husband throughout the lonely months and, despite the conflict that had plagued their marriage before he deployed, was desperate to see him again. Even so, her feelings about R&R were ambivalent at first. The goodbye back in early May had been tough on all of them, especially the boys, and she wasn't sure it was a good idea to put them all through that again. Thomas tried to turn his slot over to someone else, but his offer was refused; he was granted his 15-day R&R in mid-November.

Diane was unable to take off time from her job in the community mailroom, so when Thomas arrived back in Germany he volunteered to work with her so they wouldn't miss any time together. The days with his family seemed to reenergize Thomas, who was still reeling from his recent demotion. The reunion felt natural; in fact, it was almost a second honeymoon. Thomas jumped right up to do the dishes after dinner every evening, played with the kids for hours so that Diane had a little time for herself, and was as affectionate with her as he had been in their first months of dating. Sliding past Diane while they sorted packages in the mailroom, Thomas would give her a little pat on the rear end and steal a kiss from her when no one was looking. The days passed all too quickly.

Determined to squeeze everything in, the family celebrated Christmas early, more than a month ahead of schedule, complete with a Christmas tree and presents for everyone in the morning, followed by an early Thanksgiving dinner that same evening. The brief visit sped by and soon the time came for Thomas to return to his unit. The family shared a quiet meal together, then Thomas returned to Ramstein Air Base to catch a flight back to Iraq. Driving home with the boys, who had been dismayed to watch their father leave again, Diane unsuccessfully fought back tears. She was grateful for the dark so that her sons wouldn't see her crying.

By the end of the next day, Diane had taken down the Christmas tree and returned to her solitary existence. She was up at 6 a.m., home by 6 p.m., kids in bed by 8 p.m. But the routine no longer comforted her as it once had. In their two weeks together she had quickly adjusted to her husband's companionship, and the early morning drive to her job in the mailroom now felt unbearably empty without him.

THANKSGIVING

With the holidays fast approaching and many of her neighbors excitedly awaiting the return of their husbands for R&R, Beth was keenly aware of how little she had to look forward to in the coming months. Doug was ineligible for R&R. He had already used up all of his leave helping with her recovery and had been back in Iraq for only three weeks when the leave program was announced. There was no chance of seeing him again until the end of the deployment, still at least six months away.

This would be the second Thanksgiving in a row that Beth and Doug would be apart (he had been in basic training the year before) and she faced the holiday season with apathy. The only good thing about the holidays, Beth told herself, was that if she could somehow make it through New Year's, she would finally be on the downhill slope of the deployment.

Kathryn was now in preschool three days a week, and Beth used the time to go to the gym and to work on her online courses for the MBA program she had begun back in Phoenix. She spent most of October studying for final exams, and while she was excited to be so near to completion, she often wondered how she would fill the long, dark days of winter once she finished her degree. An avid reader, Beth ordered a constant stream of books through eBay and Books-A-Million, and the two bookshelves in her cramped living room were overflowing with Nora Roberts' historical romance novels and other light reading. Apart from books, her only other diversions from round-the-clock childcare were the phone calls from Doug that came in about once a week, TV dates with her downstairs neighbor to watch *Oprah* and *American Dreams*, and rereading the letters that Doug faithfully sent to both her and Kathryn each week. One letter she had reread so many times that she nearly had it memorized. Doug had written,

> *Dear Bethie,*
>
> *I miss you greatly and long for you to be near me.... You fill my thoughts every day, I wish there was more I could do to make things easier while I am away. I know how tired and beat up you must feel by now. With all of the challenges you have had to face since this has started, I would say you have done a remarkable job of keeping things together and taking care of Kathryn.... I love you, Bethie. I know you are tired, but please be strong for just a while longer. I know you can do it. Then I will be home and will take as much of the burden from you as possible so you can rest.*
>
> *I thank God for you every day. To have a wife who will put up [with] the things I have put you through and follow*

me around the world trying to be together. I thank you, Beth,
for the patience you have shown. I want so much for this to
end and for us to be together again! Being away from you, I
am not complete and long to be whole again.… I know you
feel as though you have not been as strong or as courageous as
you could have been, but you really have been Bethie! You
have my highest respect for what you have been through in
my absence. Thank you for being the wonderful wife that you
are.
> *With all my heart,*
> *Doug*

The letter couldn't have come at a better time. Doug was making daily trips down a dangerous route to the Baghdad airport
every day in order to collect the company mail, and Beth lived in
constant fear that something would happen to him. News of
attacks came in daily, and she woke up every morning terrified
that today might be the day that it was her husband's name in
the news articles that began, *Another soldier was killed in Iraq*
today.… Every morning she checked the Internet, praying there
wouldn't be more bad news. There were days when the fear was
paralyzing.

The weather turned dreary, and day after day Beth and
Kathryn were cooped up together in their tiny apartment with
nothing to distinguish weekdays from weekends except for
Kathryn's few hours at preschool. But November 5th was supposed
to be different. After weeks of intensive studying for final exams,
Beth was awarded an MBA from the University of Phoenix. She
had allowed herself to indulge in fantasies about the accolades
she would receive from her friends and family upon completion
of her degree, so it was a grave disappointment when the long-
anticipated day came and went with no acknowledgment from
anyone. She waited by the phone for hours, expecting a call from
Doug at any minute, but the phone never rang. Doug, whose job
in the personnel section of his battalion left him swamped with
paperwork in preparation for the R&R program, had been so busy
that he forgot about graduation day entirely. Later that afternoon,

when Beth checked her box at the community mailroom, she found that even her parents had failed to send a card. She hadn't expected a tickertape parade, but it wasn't as though she had kept the date a secret either. Graduation day had been the one event she'd had to look forward to for months, and watching it pass unnoticed shook the precarious balance she maintained between getting by and falling apart.

Doug soon realized his oversight and apologized, and his appreciative letter, which arrived shortly after the disheartening graduation day, was just the boost Beth needed to keep going. She forced herself to stop wallowing in self-pity and set about making plans for the holidays.

Thanksgiving morning dawned gray and gloomy, with dark clouds threatening a rainstorm that arrived by mid-morning. Normally Beth's Thanksgiving morning was filled with a flurry of activity to stuff the turkey and get the house in order before the guests arrived, but this year there was no need to rush. Beth knew several women who were gathering at someone's house for a home-cooked turkey dinner, but she and her downstairs neighbor, a woman with a son close to Kathryn's age and a newborn baby, had decided it would be easier to go to the Army dining facility, known as the DFAC, which was putting on a full Thanksgiving dinner for anyone holding a military ID card. Price went according to rank, so as the wife of a junior enlisted soldier Beth could have all the turkey, stuffing, and trimmings she and Kathryn could eat for only $3.25. In addition to being inexpensive, the meal was also convenient; she could leave as soon as Kathryn got tired and she wouldn't have to put on a false air of festivity.

Beth met her neighbor in the hallway at 1 p.m., pulled a raincoat over Kathryn's head, and set off for the DFAC. They had hoped to beat the crowd by going early, but by the time they got to the large stone building in the center of post, a long line of women, children, and soldiers was already winding up the stairs and around the building. The line moved surprisingly quickly, though, and soon a rear detachment soldier in his formal dress blue uniform and a paper chef's hat greeted Beth and asked to see her ID. He glanced at the card, winked at Kathryn, and said, "Free of charge," allowing them both to pass into the cafeteria-style food line without paying even the marginal entrance fee.

"I guess there are some benefits to being at the low end of the totem pole," Beth commented wryly.

Inside the DFAC was a whirlwind of activity. The room was brightly lit and cheerfully decorated, and were it not for the haggard expressions worn on many women's faces and the peculiar absence of fathers, it might have seemed like any other Army-sponsored social gathering. Apart from a few tables full of single soldiers who had only recently arrived on post and had not yet been sent down to their new units in Iraq, most tables were filled with groups of casually dressed women and young children. A clown kept throngs of excited toddlers entertained in one corner, doling out animal-shaped balloons, while mothers carried trays heaped with applesauce, turkey, mashed potatoes, and pumpkin pie back to their tables.

Between chasing after Kathryn and helping with her friend's baby, Beth barely had a chance to sit down to eat her meal, not that she minded. She grimaced as she poked at the overcooked turkey and heavily salted stuffing, sighing, "Well, at least there isn't anything to clean up." As soon as Kathryn was fed and had collected her balloon Beth decided it was time to leave, foregoing a stop with the camera crew outside. The Army had hired a production company to make a videotape of Thanksgiving Day activities at eight of its dining halls, and Baumholder was one of them. Spouses and children could deliver a personal message to deployed troops, which would later be distributed to the soldiers downrange. But Beth had nothing she wanted to say to Doug that she was willing to share with a thousand other soldiers, so instead she bundled up Kathryn and headed home; by two o'clock her Thanksgiving was over.

During the daylight hours she hadn't minded being alone on Thanksgiving; it had felt like any other day. But that evening, when her family began to call, feelings of despondency welled up inside her. When her mother called to excitedly tell Beth about the family's preparations for Thanksgiving dinner at an aunt's house, it only made Beth feel more isolated. Later that evening a cousin called to express her delight that President Bush had flown to Iraq unannounced to have Thanksgiving dinner with the troops.

"Isn't it so great that he did that!" her cousin gushed. Beth couldn't answer honestly. Her honest answer would have been that she was appalled by the news footage of the president standing amidst the troops at Baghdad International Airport, holding up a turkey and joking, "I was just looking for a warm meal somewhere." As far as Beth was concerned, if the president really wanted to do something nice for the troops, then he should send them home. Don't you get it? she thought as she hung up the phone. Don't tell me how great it is that the president is in Baghdad when I spent the day eating slimy turkey in the mess hall by myself!

Across post at Teresa's apartment, a very different Thanksgiving celebration was taking place. Weeks earlier Teresa, Heather, and Jennifer had decided to go all out for the holiday with a traditional, home-cooked feast followed by a slumber party. They invited the whole gang from Buddy Night and spent Thanksgiving morning arranging a borrowed picnic table and extra mattresses so that everyone would have a place to eat and sleep. All the guests had agreed to contribute something to the meal: Jennifer brought mashed potatoes and a salad, Heather made her grandmother's "famous" Louisiana dressing, another friend prepared a sweet potato soufflé, and Teresa, apart from hosting the evening, volunteered to provide a turkey, low-carb stuffing for the dieters, and pies.

With Heather and Jennifer's help the early preparations went smoothly, but when Teresa started working on the pies, she quickly found herself in over her head. Over and over she smeared the rolling pin with flour, placed the mound of dough in the center of the counter, and began what seemed like a simple process, but each time she tried to roll out the glob of dough it either fell apart or stuck to everything in sight. She was about ready to throw in the towel and send someone off to the commissary to pick up some Sara Lee when the phone rang.

"Danny!" she squealed in delight, clutching the phone between her ear and shoulder as she scraped the sticky mass of dough off her hands and forearms. "Happy Thanksgiving! I'm so glad you called!" Danny told her about his Thanksgiving plans. He had a patrol scheduled for later in the day, but at least when he and his guys got back they would have a good meal waiting for them. The mess hall was putting on Thanksgiving dinner and the commanders were serving it up. All things considered, it wasn't so bad; certainly better than last year when he'd been stuck on a training mission in eastern Germany, shivering and up to his knees in half-frozen muck. Once they were caught up Teresa confessed that she was especially glad that he had called, not only because she was relieved, as always, to hear his voice, but also because she was desperately in need of his culinary assistance. Of the two of them, Danny was by far the better cook, and if there was any hope of salvaging dessert his well-timed phone call was it.

Danny explained how to get the dough into the proper consistency and reminded her about the finicky nature of their oven. "Remember to turn the pies," he cautioned. "Otherwise one side will be raw and the other will be burned to a crisp." Teresa followed his advice, and the pies were a success.

Most of the guests arrived by mid-afternoon, bringing with them snacks, board games, and enough vodka and sour apple mix for multiple rounds of apple martinis. Teresa had insisted that the dinner be a dress down affair and the dinner guests followed her instructions in unabashed comfort, padding through the apartment in their socks, poking fingers into Teresa's cooling pies, and taking turns as bartender.

When the time came to sit down to dinner the friends clasped hands as Nancy, a captain's wife in the battalion, led the prayer. "Dear Lord," she began with her head bowed. "We give thanks for the wonderful food and friends gathered here today. With our husbands far away and in constant danger, this is a difficult Thanksgiving for all of us, but without the support of the incredible women here today it would be even harder."

Several of the dinner guests murmured their agreement, and Nancy waited until the room was silent again before she continued, "We are all so grateful to you for protecting our husbands and keeping them out of harm's way. We pray that you will continue to watch over them. Please, Lord, keep them safe and bring them home. Amen."

"Amen," everyone replied amidst sniffles and nervous laughter.

"Okay, could we please have just one day without crying?" Teresa pleaded as she dabbed at her own eyes. "Let's eat!"

They talked and laughed and drank and ate until the food was almost gone, joking that the one upside of a deployment was that they could stuff themselves to the gills so long as they slimmed back down before their husbands came home. Once they could eat no more, they mixed up another round of cocktails, changed into their pajamas, and gathered in the living room for games. They started with Malarky, a game in which the players try to determine the truth when faced with a set of both real and completely made up answers to questions such as "Why are pistachios dyed red?" One of Teresa's dinner guests, a diminutive Philappina unaccustomed to alcohol, passed out on the couch only to awake at odd intervals shouting, "Malarky!" and sending the rest of the group into fits of raucous laughter.

The hours passed quickly and the next thing they knew it was past two o'clock in the morning. The guests retired and soon the apartment was quiet, filled with sleeping women who, for the first time in months, did not go to sleep alone.

WINTER

This year's Iraq war wrenched more servicemembers from their families over the holidays than in any year since 1990, creating 180,000 blue Christmases at U.S. military bases around the world.

—Stars and Stripes[1]

CHAPTER NINE

"Ladies and gentlemen, we got him."
— *U.S. Administrator L. Paul Bremmer
announces the capture of Saddam Hussein.
U.S. forces captured the former Iraqi dictator
Saturday, December 13, 2003
in a cellar outside the town of Tikrit.*

"CAUGHT LIKE A RAT"

On December 14th, when people in Baumholder checked the headlines, they were greeted with the first good news many had seen in weeks: a dirty, disheveled Saddam Hussein had been captured and was now in American custody. Soldiers from the 1st Brigade Combat Team of the 4th Infantry Division and special operations forces had found the former Iraqi dictator hiding in a "six- to eight-foot hole" outside his hometown of Tikrit. Major General Raymond Odierno, the 4th Infantry Division commander, told reporters, "He was in the bottom of a hole with no way to fight back. He was just caught like a rat." Phones rang off the hook as excited friends and family members called to share the good news, and everyone wondered what the long-sought-after capture might mean for the future of the occupation. The next day the *Stars and Stripes,* a Department of Defense-authorized daily newspaper widely read in overseas military communities, reported from Baumholder, "At this Army base where more than 5,000 troops are currently deployed to Iraq, the reaction to Saddam's capture was a mixture of pride, relief, cautious celebration, and a perhaps-unrealistic hope that it will bring local soldiers home."[1]

The newspaper might well have been describing Teresa, who felt sure the capture would speed Danny's homecoming. For the first time in the terrifying and often disappointing occupation, it finally seemed like the soldiers were making progress. That evening, a dinner party that originally had been planned as a send off for all the women who were spending Christmas and New Year's back in the States morphed into an impromptu "We Got Saddam!" celebration. Heather arrived grinning ear-to-ear, eager to show off a brand new t-shirt emblazoned with a Hard Rock Café-style design that read *Baghdad: Under New Management*. The capture of Saddam Hussein made that brazen statement finally seem true, and each time the gaunt, disheveled former dictator's image appeared on television the friends let out whoops and cheers. Even the more cynical military wives in the group allowed themselves to feel hopeful; after so many anxious months, it felt good to have a reason for optimism.

While many on post shared Teresa's enthusiasm, others saw the capture of the former Iraqi dictator as a positive development that would, unfortunately, make little difference in the situation on the ground. From her former career in military intelligence, Tasha knew that the excitement many of her peers felt was over-blown; whether Saddam Hussein was in U.S. custody or not, her husband was not coming home any sooner. "I couldn't care less one way or the other," she remarked offhandedly as she observed footage of Iraqis shooting guns into the air in celebration on the streets of Baghdad. Sure, she got a little thrill from the *way* he was captured, lying in a rat hole. But would the capture of Saddam Hussein affect the big picture? She didn't think so. The capture didn't change the fact that many of Saddam's former subjects clearly saw the American troops as occupiers instead of libera-tors and would go to any length to force them out of the country. It didn't change the fact that if the soldiers pulled out of Iraq right now, the result would probably be civil war. And it certainly didn't change the fact that the Iraqi insurgents were carrying out more deadly attacks against U.S. troops than ever. "President Bush says a tyrant has been taken down," she stated hotly, "but [Saddam Hussein is] not the one shooting at us!"

As she talked, her attention was diverted by a grim-faced reporter who had appeared on the television screen that continuously hummed in Tasha's living room, announcing that a helicopter had gone down in Iraq, killing all eight U.S. soldiers aboard. Tasha leaned forward, her hands grasping the sides of the leather recliner. She listened intently as the reporter gave a few sketchy details: the pilot had been attempting a crash landing, the helicopter went down near Fallujah, eight servicemen had been killed.... An anchorwoman nodded sympathetically when the reporter finished speaking, then moved on to the next segment, a curiosity piece about a young man who was shot in the head with a nail gun and lived to tell about it. Tasha turned away from the television set in disgust and asked angrily, "What are we supposed to do?" Her question hung in the air, unanswered.

FELIZ NAVIDAD Y PRÓSPERO AÑO NUEVO

Meanwhile, Teresa's initial enthusiasm about Saddam Hussein's capture had been dampened by a conversation she had with Danny the day after the much celebrated event, who told her that whether Saddam was in U.S. custody or not, nearly insurmountable problems remained in the country; there was no way he was going to get home any sooner as a result of the capture.

The next day she flew to California to spend Christmas and New Year's Eve with her family, and as the plane pulled up to the gate at LAX, she tried to imagine what the Christmas holiday would be like without Danny. It was impossible to pretend that everything was normal when he was in mortal danger every minute of the day. He was supposed to be with her, playing with the nieces and nephews who idolized him and running out the door on Christmas Eve to buy a few last-minute Christmas presents. Overwhelmed by the excitement and then disappointment of Saddam Hussein's capture and the emotional tug of the holiday season, Teresa had felt dangerously close to tears ever since boarding the plane, and she told herself that she had to keep it together during the visit. She knew she had worried her parents enough during their disastrous summer visit and she wanted to reassure them that, no matter how bad things had been over the summer and no matter how much she still missed Danny, she was doing okay now.

The incomplete family reunion was a relief on both sides: Teresa was grateful to be mothered for a while, and her family was elated to see Teresa back to her usual, plucky self. Teresa visited Danny's parents and tried in vain to comfort her mother-in-law, who was having just as hard a time dealing with the fact that Danny was in Iraq as she was, but Teresa didn't know what to say and soon returned to the comfort of her own family, running errands and relaxing.

A few days into the visit Teresa and her mother visited a fabric store, hoping to find material to cover an antique bench that Teresa had recently purchased in Germany. Teresa quickly found what she wanted and took it up to the cash register to pay, handing the clerk her credit card and military ID. The clerk examined the card closely. "Are you a soldier?" she asked Teresa.

"No, no," she replied with a laugh. Danny often kidded her that, with her quick temper, she would be a disaster waiting to happen if anyone was foolish enough to put a gun in her hands. "My husband is a soldier. He's in Iraq."

The clerk nodded, and as she finalized the purchase she said, "I want to thank you and your husband for all that you do."

Teresa was caught off guard by the stranger's thanks. It had never occurred to her that anyone in her Southern California town —a place that seemed worlds away from the war in Iraq—would care at all about the soldiers and their families. Being included in the clerk's thanks especially touched Teresa because it had seemed to her that few people recognized that the soldiers were not going through the deployment alone, that their spouses and children and parents were going through something very difficult too.

As they gathered their packages, Teresa's mother noticed the tears forming in her daughter's eyes.

"Que pasó, mija?" she asked Teresa, wanting to know what had made her cry.

Teresa, rendered speechless by the unexpected words of kindness, hurried her mother out of the store so that she could collect herself in private before she explained.

That evening Teresa huddled in her old bedroom with two of her sisters. "I have something to show you," she whispered conspiratorially. "But you have to promise not to laugh. I need you to help me choose which of these to put into the album for Danny's birthday." She opened her suitcase and handed her sisters a pack of photographs.

"Oh my God!" one sister shouted gleefully. "You got them!"

The idea to pose for seductive photos to send to Danny had come about a month earlier. Heather was the first to do it, and had turned up in Teresa's office one afternoon with an entire album of photos of herself posed in an array of Victoria's Secret lingerie. Jennifer's photo shoot was next, and Teresa came along to do her make-up and give moral support. As Jennifer posed nervously in front of the camera Teresa stood in the wings, whistling and egging her on by shouting, "Come on! You're supposed to look sexy!" and "I better see some boobs!" Jennifer scowled in response before bursting into laughter, holding out her wine glass for another dose of liquid courage. One by one, all the friends from Buddy Night took the plunge, poring over Victoria's Secret catalogs to choose just the right look. And at every photo shoot, Teresa was there, cheering from the sidelines.

When Teresa's lingerie purchases arrived, she raced over to Jennifer's apartment to show her the loot. Shying away from anything too provocative that would only draw attention to what she describes as her "non-existent figure," she had chosen several bra and boy short combinations, all offering more coverage than an average bikini, and what had looked in the catalog like a silky peach shorts and tank set. But when she pulled it out of the package she realized in horror that it was completely see-through.

"No way," she told Jennifer. "I am *not* wearing anything see-through."

"Oh yes you are," Jennifer told her. "What happened to Miss 'show me your boobs'? You're wearing it."

On the day of her photo shoot, Teresa packed up her new lingerie as well as a beautiful red satin ball gown she had worn to a formal at West Point and a conservative white nightgown her mother had always said she looked pretty in, and met Heather and Jennifer at the photo studio. In the dressing room, she stripped down to her bra and underwear and examined the peach shorts set anxiously. If I have to wear something see-through, she decided, I am keeping my underwear on. She slid the outfit on top of her sensible, un-sexy undergarments, and exited the dressing room with her arms across her chest. Heather and Jennifer howled with laughter at the sight of her.

"So you can dish it out when it's our turn," Heather laughed, "but look what happens when it's you in front of the camera! You're all talk!"

"Shut up," Teresa said.

Just then the photographer, a young, enlisted soldier's wife with a no-nonsense sense of humor who had gotten to know the group well in previous weeks, walked in. "You're not actually going to wear that, are you?" she asked Teresa incredulously.

Teresa returned to the dressing room and emerged moments later in her white nightgown. Making the ugliest face possible she said, "Okay. I'm ready now."

She had gotten the photos back a few days before her trip to California and watched closely as her sisters examined each one, selecting some of the sexier shots in lingerie and a couple elegant photographs in her red satin gown. But their favorite, and the only one that truly looked like her, they said, was the one in the white "granny-style" nightgown, making an ugly face.

"Now this one," Teresa's older sister pronounced, "This one is you." Teresa agreed, sliding the photo into the first slot of the photo album.

Christmas arrived soon afterward, and the extended family—brothers, sisters, in-laws, nieces, and nephews—gathered together around the Christmas tree to open their presents, including gifts that Danny had somehow managed to find between his busy patrolling schedule and other responsibilities as platoon leader. Teresa's father got a pair of Iraqi-style sandals; her mother a bracelet; her sister an ornately carved teapot; and Teresa received a beautiful set of earrings, a necklace, and a bracelet. But the real highlight of Christmas morning was when Teresa's niece and nephew opened up their gifts from Danny. The little boy opened up his present first, revealing one of the floppy, camouflaged hats worn by soldiers in the desert with his name embroidered on the front in Arabic. "Cool!" he exclaimed, showing it off to everyone in the room. Teresa's five-year-old niece, a "girlie girl" who had always favored Danny above her other relatives, opened her gift next, her big brown eyes gleaming with anticipation. She lifted up a fancy jewelry box, trimmed with delicate metalwork, and held it up to her brother as if to say, See? I got something great, too. She then went up to the camera that had followed every moment of Christmas morning so that Danny could later participate in absentia and thanked him for the present.

"Thank you, Uncle Danny," she said sweetly. "I love you."

Everyone took a turn on camera to say something to Danny, and there was little variation in the messages: They loved him and missed him and wanted him to come home soon. Watching them speak, Teresa saw how deep their feelings were for her husband, and how close they, too, were to tears. For the second time in the visit, Teresa broke the promise she had made to herself not to cry.

For Teresa, the weeks with her family allowed her to return to a more innocent time of life. Even after his four years at West Point and several years in the Army, her family still had a hard time grasping the fact that Danny was a soldier, and they looked incredulously at photos of him in his desert combat uniform. They still remembered him as her high school sweetheart, a fun-loving jokester teasing Teresa relentlessly and making everyone laugh, not a tough soldier carrying a gun and leading men in a war zone. Teresa liked being reminded of those simpler times, times when she didn't watch the news in terror; times when images of explosions didn't fill her dreams.

THE CHRISTMAS VISIT

Back in Baumholder, on the day Teresa left for California, Jena raced around her apartment, getting everything ready for Adam's imminent arrival. She had not expected to see him until spring.

As a low-ranking private with no children or marital problems, she had assumed that he would be last on the R&R list. In fact, Adam had asked to be put there. He knew his marriage was strong and that Jena was coping well with the deployment, and thought it was only fair that someone else who needed the break more than he did get the chance to go home. But the first sergeant had put Adam's name into the lottery along with the rest, and shortly after Thanksgiving he had found out that he was coming home December 14th, in time for both Christmas and their fourth wedding anniversary.

Adam was right to assume that Jena was coping with the deployment well. Like other spouses in Baumholder, she had days when she was overcome by worry and couldn't look away from the disturbing scenes on CNN, but overall she had found a contented, meaningful life for herself in Baumholder, even if Adam couldn't be a part of it at the moment. Jena saw too many of her friends and neighbors putting their lives on hold during the deployment, and she thought it was a big mistake. It wasn't healthy, and it certainly didn't help the soldiers. "It's good for them to know you miss them," she theorized, "but not for them to think you miss them *too* much."

During her months alone, Jena had completed some of the items on the to-do list she had written out just after Adam left, namely fun trips to Poland and Italy, but others remained, such as organizing their storage area and starting a scrap-booking project of the deployment. The projects kept her focused on the present, not just wishing the year away. They also helped to pass the time; instead of viewing Adam's return as an eternity away, she thought of all projects she wanted to get done before he came back, and wondered how she would ever find the time.[2]

At first, Jena was nervous when she found out about R&R. She worried that things between them might be different, that the months in Iraq might have changed Adam or that she would fall apart when she watched him leave again. She shared her concerns with her best friend in Baumholder, a more experienced Army spouse, who cautioned her that she was thinking about it all wrong. "It's not about you," her friend told her. "It's about him."

It was so obvious; why hadn't she thought of it that way before? *He* was the one facing life and death situations day in and day out, not her. And if he was going to get through the final months of the deployment safely, he needed some time away from it all. Looking at it that way eased Jena's concerns. All she had to do was make sure that Adam's needs were taken care of during the visit and the rest would fall into place.

On the day Adam was due to arrive in Germany, Jena drove to the airport well ahead of his scheduled 1 a.m. arrival time, but when she got there, she learned that the flight had been delayed for hours. Fearing that she might miss the arrival if she left the airport, she settled in on the floor and tried to sleep. When the plane finally landed at 8 a.m., she and two other exhausted Army wives rushed to the waiting area to meet their husbands. A chaplain came out first and informed them that their husbands were on their way to the meeting area, but that they were required to go through a mandatory 15-minute briefing and that until that briefing had taken place, there should be no physical contact between husbands and wives. Jena wondered how she would manage to restrain herself, but her self-control was never tested; as soon as Adam appeared he went straight to her.

"I don't care what the rules are," he whispered, and drew her in for a kiss.

On the drive home she couldn't stop staring at him. For so many months the closest she had been able to get to Adam was a white cordless phone. Jena kept two phones, one reserved for Adam and one for everyone else, so that when the phone that she carried with her everywhere rang, she knew immediately that it was her husband. All this time that was all he had been to her: a voice on a scratchy telephone line every seven to ten days for twenty minutes or so at a stretch, if she was lucky. But now here he was, sitting beside her. It was strange; she knew he was her husband, but somehow he still didn't seem real.

The next morning, Adam woke up at 4 a.m. He was restless and couldn't sleep; he needed to get out of the apartment. Jena dragged herself out of their warm bed and kept him company as he drove out to the autobahn, cruising aimlessly in the predawn hours. When they finally returned home they spent the day quietly: they took the dog out for a long walk in the woods behind their apartment building, watched videos, and caught up with their families. Jena made sure that everything was very calm, and she hoped that soon Adam would relax enough to be able to sleep in. But all throughout his first week at home Adam awoke, restless and agitated, well before dawn.

Jena could see that Adam had changed during his time in Iraq. Having witnessed the deprivation with which most Iraqis lived, and having been deprived of many commonplace luxuries himself, he had a greater appreciation of how much Americans took for granted. The hot shower in their apartment now seemed the height of decadence. But other experiences he'd had in Iraq were more troubling. In Adam's family, for instance, the men were taught to idealize women and put them up on pedestals. In Iraq, the women Adam had seen were treated much differently, and their subservient role in society was difficult for him to understand and accept. More disturbingly, he had seen the effects of violence close up: His unit had been the first on the scene at the deadly bombing of a Red Cross building. He had watched people die; he had pulled away charred body parts burned beyond recognition. As Jena listened silently to his stories, she thought sadly that no one could experience something like that and not be changed by it.

Jena never asked a lot of questions when Adam talked about Iraq; she knew that he would tell her everything in his own time. They had always been completely open with one another, and had promised to always try to understand whatever the other one had to say, no matter how difficult. They had no secrets that she was aware of, and in their almost four years of marriage they had never had a telephone conversation behind closed doors. So Jena was stunned when, one evening, Adam picked up the phone to call his grandfather, walked into the bedroom, and shut the door behind him.

Jena busied herself by taking the dog for a walk, washing dishes, anything to keep from staring at the clock and wondering what in the world he was saying that he didn't want her to hear.

Meanwhile, behind the closed door, Adam talked softly with his grandfather, a World War II veteran, probing him for answers to the multitude of questions that were the source of his 4 a.m. restlessness. When will the images of those burned body parts go away? As a Christian, do the things I did in Iraq violate my faith? Will my wife think less of me when I tell her what I have seen and done? How can I tell her that I have shot at people?

Much later, after a long conversation with his grandfather, Adam went into the kitchen and wrapped his arms around Jena. He knew he had hurt her by shutting her out of his conversation, and he wanted to explain. In part, he said, he had needed to talk privately with someone who had been through it, or at least someone who had been through a similar experience. But more than that, he had feared that if she knew everything she wouldn't see him the way she once had, that she might look down on him or feel that he was no longer the decent man she had married.

For the first time in their relationship, Jena realized, there were things that Adam might never be able to share with her, things she could not begin to comprehend. It wasn't like before when the most upsetting event of the day was bad traffic or a boss's unfair decision. This was a whole new dimension, one she hadn't anticipated, and she realized that the only choice she had was to accept it.

Christmas soon approached and Jena was filled with memories of their first Christmas as a married couple. They had been inundated with houseguests, and the crowded household made it nearly impossible to carry out their plan of putting up their Christmas tree alone together, without the chaos of small nieces and nephews and cousins underfoot. Christmas was nearly upon them and they still had no tree. Then, late one night, Adam roused Jena from her sleep and brought his yawning wife into the living room. Secretly, he had set up the tree, and together they set about stringing up lights and adding decorations. When it was all done they cuddled up on the couch together in the dark room, lit only by the twinkling Christmas tree lights, and admired their work. Since that year, the 2 a.m. tree trimmings had become a tradition, both Adam and Jena more than willing to trade a restful night's sleep for the intimacy of trimming a tree when, as Jena put it, "the world is asleep."

This year, much to Jena's surprise and delight, was no exception. One night before Christmas Adam slid out of bed to set up the tree, then returned to the bedroom and watched Jena for a few moments as she slumbered, her index finger tucked inside his wedding band, which she wore on a necklace for safe keeping. Then he woke her so their annual Christmas ritual could begin.

Just after Christmas, Adam packed up the blanket she had given him as a fourth anniversary present—a hand-made quilt she had patched together from pieces of cloth from their wedding, honeymoon, and other travels together—and prepared to return to Iraq. He was in a visibly improved frame of mind by then, rested and more relaxed, finally able to sleep through the night. He was ready to go back and talked often of his guilt about being away from his responsibilities and platoon buddies. Although Jena was sad to see him go, her overwhelming feeling as she steeled herself for another goodbye was one of gratitude. I could have gone the whole 12 months if I had to, she thought, but for Adam, the break from the relentless stress of life in Iraq had been an absolute necessity.

CHAPTER TEN

"Military duty doesn't damage relationships so much as it tests them. Those that are not firmly in place can be broken by the absences and the weaknesses that are exacerbated for the relationship during those times."
—*Lt. Col. Robert Strayhan, M.D.,*
associate professor at the
University of South Dakota Medical School

KEISHA'S CHRISTMAS ANGELS

Tasha did not want a Christmas tree this year. There was no sense celebrating Christmas with Anthony in Iraq, and if she had her way she would have fallen asleep the day before Thanksgiving and woken up on New Year's Day. But eventually she gave in to Keisha's relentless pleading and agreed to take the artificial tree out of its box in the corner of the living room, where it had sat since just after Thanksgiving, and set it up. She drew the line at decorating it, though, and told Keisha that if she wanted the tree decorated, she would have to do it herself.

Keisha began with their small collection of Christmas angels and then expanded the theme when she found a box of angel ornaments on sale at the PX. Keisha announced that the angels were meant to bring her stepfather back safely from Iraq, and every week Tasha noticed that more and more angels covered the tree. Keisha said that she didn't intend to take the tree and its talismans down until Anthony came home safely.

Tasha and Keisha spent the holiday quietly. They went to church, ate a late dinner, and watched videos until they both fell asleep in front of the television. Christmas came and went uneventfully, then New Year's, and still the tree remained in the corner of the living room, the branches pulled lower and lower as Keisha added angels.

If she was true to her word, the tree was going to be up for a long time. Anthony had lost out in the R&R lottery and although Tasha tried to convince herself it was better for her that way, that it would have been too hard to watch him leave again, the fact that he was not coming home was a sore spot. Tasha knew how exhausted her husband was; his platoon was so short on NCOs that he rarely got any time off, and he had patrolled on Christmas day, New Year's Eve, and most days in between. A recurrent problem with his knees had flared up again, and he told Tasha in a recent phone call that he had been "popping Motrin like candy." He needed a break, if not back at home then somewhere down there, and Tasha was furious that no one in his chain of command seemed to recognize that. "I hurt for him," she said, shaking her head sadly. "I'm tired for him. When is this nightmare going to end?"

It was hard enough for Tasha to watch her neighbors' husbands coming home, to have to walk past signs in her stairwell that read *Welcome Home, Daddy!* and *We Missed You!*, knowing that her own husband would not return for months, but it was even harder to observe the reunited couples fighting. All she heard, it seemed, were stories about R&R disasters, the worst of which involved a soldier who had come home from Iraq only to find his wife heading off on vacation with her new boyfriend. According to the Baumholder rumor mill, the jilted husband responded by totaling their new car and spent the rest of his 15 days of what was supposed to be rest and recuperation alone, crying in his apartment. Two weeks later he was on a plane back to Baghdad. Hearing those stories made Tasha want to yell, *Send* my *husband back!* She wouldn't have wasted a minute of her time fighting with Anthony, not that she was going to get the chance to prove that. "The people in dire situations and [with new] babies get to see their husbands," she said, "but the rest of us? They just leave us hanging."

A STRANGER COMES HOME

Kristina and Scott were not exactly in a dire situation— Kristina had never considered walking out on her marriage or imperiling it with an affair—but the bond she and Scott once shared had eroded during the long months of separation. So much so that when Scott called in late January to tell her that he was finally scheduled to fly out the next morning for R&R, Kristina had no idea how to respond to the news. She was thrilled that Marie and Tyler were going to get to spend some time with their father but was hesitant about their own reunion. She felt certain they were going to fight, that he would criticize her parenting and financial decisions, that he wouldn't approve of the changes she had made in the apartment, or that he might question her faithfulness to him while he was gone as he had during previous separations.

They didn't have a great track record with deployments; in fact, the first deployment they had experienced as a couple had nearly ended their relationship. Only weeks into their romance, Scott was sent on a three-month mission in Albania. Kristina had thought of little else while he was gone, and on the day of his anxiously awaited homecoming she arrived at the Army post several hours early, two friends in tow to help her through the final, excruciating wait.

Scott's bus was delayed for hours, and with nowhere else to go, Kristina and her friends remained seated on the increasingly chilly cement curb in front of the barracks. A few single soldiers who lived inside invited the young women in for a cup of coffee and a couch to sit on while they waited, and they gratefully accepted the seemingly harmless offer. The soldiers regaled them with wild stories of military blunders and heroics, both heavily seasoned with exaggerations and wishful thinking, while Kristina impatiently checked her watch.

Hours passed and the young women eventually returned to the curb where Kristina, exhausted from anticipation and lack of sleep, was just beginning to nod off when her friend nudged her. "Kristina," her friend whispered. "Kristina!" she said again, louder this time. "Die Busse Kommen!"

"Sind sie hier?" Kristina asked groggily, rubbing her eyes and trying to focus. She had a vague notion of men in green uniforms walking toward the barracks but, still more asleep than awake, couldn't quite process the information. She remained motionless. Her friend nudged her again, and Kristina looked up to see a tall, frowning young man staring down at her.

"Scott!" she shouted, suddenly wide-awake, but when she hugged him she was met with a stiff response.

"I thought you'd be glad to see me," Scott said, visibly disappointed by what seemed like a less than enthusiastic greeting.

"Of course I'm glad to see you!" she exclaimed. "I'm just so tired. I've been sitting here all night." Scott said nothing further and Kristina assumed the matter was forgotten. But the next day, when Scott returned to the barracks, some unwelcome news awaited him.

The soldiers who had invited Kristina and her friends into the barracks had their own version of the events that night, a version they shared with Scott as soon as he dumped his rucksack on the floor of his small barracks room. One soldier, an infamous "player" who was known to keep a tally of his sexual conquests, told Scott that Kristina had come on to him, and that it was only out of respect for his fellow soldier that he had ignored her advances; he thought Scott had a right to know.

It was months before Kristina was able to convince Scott that nothing had happened that night, that she hadn't *wanted* anything to happen. She would have to be a complete idiot to make a move on a soldier in Scott's own unit the night he was coming home, she told him, and besides, the guy wasn't even her type. "I love you, Scott," she said. "I never want to be with anyone else."

Grudgingly, Scott accepted her denials, but the seed of doubt that was planted that night had remained a nagging issue throughout their engagement and marriage. Scott bristled any time he caught other soldiers eyeing her approvingly, and Kristina knew that, even though she had never given him cause for concern, Scott still harbored deep suspicions about what she did in his absence. There was no better breeding ground for paranoia than Iraq.

But even if Scott didn't launch any insane accusations, there were other problems in the marriage now that could not be avoided. Kristina had built up a lot of resentment toward Scott during the deployment. In all the time he had been gone he had sent only three letters, he almost never called, and even though he now had regular access to email, he rarely checked his messages and sent even fewer. There were days when she wanted so badly to be able to tell him she loved him and that she missed him but, she thought dejectedly, she might as well tell it to the wall.

Even Scott's rare phone calls did little to lessen the void. It seemed as though their friendship had disappeared, that instead of sharing their feelings as they once had, they buried them. During a recent call she had tried to open up to him, only to have the door slammed in her face.

"I miss you so much, babe," she had said. "And the kids miss you, too. You should have heard Marie the other day..."

Scott had cut her off before she could finish her sentence. "That's the last thing I need to hear, Kristina. Hearing that sort of thing only makes life more difficult for me."

Fine, Kristina had thought angrily. I won't tell you. I won't tell you anything. Since then, the emotional wall she had reluctantly begun to build over the summer had grown higher, and she had little hope that two short weeks together would be enough to tear it down.

The day after Scott's call telling her that he was on his way home, Kristina scoured the apartment, put fresh sheets on the bed, and carefully chose an outfit to wear for his arrival. She then took the kids out to window shop in downtown Baumholder, played computer games, surfed the net, anything to pass the time. That night, as she often did, she went to bed with the phone, and for the first time in more than eight months she prayed it wouldn't ring; a phone call so close to Scott's departure time would probably mean there had been another delay. By the next morning she had still heard nothing. She passed another restless day, and again went to bed with the phone, certain he would be home by morning. She planned to wake up early, get dressed looking her best, and then nap on the couch until he called to tell her he was back in Germany.

At 4:30 in the morning, Kristina was awoken by what sounded like a knock on the door. She stumbled out of bed in her pajamas —a loose t-shirt and gym shorts—no makeup on, her hair disheveled, and went to investigate. She peered through the peephole but saw no one there, and was about to return to bed when she heard the knock again. She opened the door to find Scott standing in the hallway, soaking wet from rain and wearing a big grin on his face. Startled and still half asleep, Kristina jumped behind the door and tried to close it, not wanting her husband's first glimpse of her to be so decidedly unglamorous. Scott pushed the door open and said, laughing, "Well that's a hell of a welcome!"

Kristina put on a pot of coffee and they sat together on the couch, updating one another on all their recent news. But as hard as she tried to act natural, the conversation felt forced. Scott looked like her husband, but he felt like a stranger.

Later that morning Scott took a long bath—getting out eight months of sand, he said—while Kristina checked on the kids. She was worried about how Marie and Tyler would react to seeing their father again. Tyler had been so little when Scott left that she felt certain he wouldn't recognize his father now, and she knew Marie was hurt and confused by her father's continuing absence. No matter how many ways Kristina tried to explain the situation to her daughter, she knew she didn't really understand.

Only two days earlier, when Scott had failed to arrive as Kristina had promised he would, the little girl had remarked sullenly, "I don't want my daddy to come home." Kristina knew that Marie was only verbalizing an entirely understandable frustration, but feared that when she saw her father for the first time she might not give him the warm reception he was expecting. Hoping to rekindle Marie's enthusiasm, Kristina had given her a bright silver helium balloon—a special welcome home present for Daddy just from her—and instructed Marie to hide it in the closet as a surprise.

Scott was toweling himself off when Marie woke up. She must have heard his voice, because she marched out of her room, still draped in one of Scott's old Army t-shirts, balloon in hand, and went straight to the bathroom. Handing her father the balloon, she said, "Here Daddy. It's a surprise for you." Scott took the balloon and asked if he could have a hug and kiss. Marie reached up her arms to her father and didn't let go for minutes; it was as if he had never been gone at all. Tyler also seemed at ease with Scott, falling asleep in his father's arms only days into the visit.

Kristina was tremendously relieved. She knew how scared Scott had been that his children wouldn't remember him, or that they would resent him for leaving them. She also knew how much he had missed them while he was in Iraq. Several weeks ago, he told her that morning, he and some other soldiers had been listening to the radio and playing cards when the song "I'm Already There" came on the air. The song was a musical tribute to deployed soldiers by the country band Lone Star. At one point in the sentimental ballad, a recording of a small child welcoming a deployed father home is played. "Daddy!" the child cries out, and although Scott had heard the song countless times before and usually thought it was cheesy, on that particular day hearing a child's voice saying the word *daddy* got to him, and a tear slid down his cheek. The other soldiers noticed and razzed him about it, but Scott, who saw nothing to be ashamed of, simply replied, "You don't know what it's like to be a dad."

Over the next few days, Scott got up early to take care of the kids in the morning, letting Kristina sleep in for the first time in months. He made an effort to divide his time equally between his two children, making sure that neither felt left out while he was occupied with the other. He couldn't get over how much they had changed in the time he had been gone. Tyler had been a tiny three-month-old baby when he left, who did nothing more interesting than sleep, eat, and wet himself, but now he was an actual little person who moved on his own and was beginning to display his own personality. Marie had changed a lot as well. She had barely spoken in sentences eight months earlier, but now she rattled on incessantly in her greatly expanded vocabulary, both in English and German. "She speaks more German than I do!" Scott exclaimed.

The visit with Tyler and Marie was going better than Kristina had ever dreamed, but her own reunion with Scott remained strained. They had not fought, as she had feared they would, and although Scott had made a few references to tales of cheating wives he had heard from his buddies, he had not directly accused her of anything. They had even been able to joke about some of the more ridiculous rumors flying around post. He liked the new curtains she had hung in the living room, complemented her on the money she had managed to save, and voiced only minor complaints about her decision to put the kids in day care a few hours a week. They were considerate of one another and managed to maintain the appearance of a happily reunited couple, but still it felt hollow. Kristina was only going through the motions of being a loving, affectionate wife; none of it felt real.

Several days into R&R, Kristina and Scott woke up simultaneously in the middle of the night. Scott turned to her, rubbing her arm gently to see if she was awake, and Kristina rolled over to face him.

"Do you still feel close to me?" he asked, examining her face. "I'm asking because I can't shake the feeling that, even though we're physically close, it isn't close enough. I feel like I can't get close to you. I want to, but I can't, and I don't know why."

Kristina was momentarily speechless; he had just said exactly what she had been feeling since he arrived. "Yeah, I know what you mean," she said, her bottom lip shaking as she started to cry. Scott wrapped his arms around her and pulled her into his chest, wiping away the tears as they streamed down her cheeks. They stayed up the rest of the night talking, crying, holding each other, slowly starting to reconnect.

After that night, Kristina and Scott began talking openly for the first time about how poorly they had communicated during his absence. Scott had minimized communication with her intentionally, he explained. A higher ranking soldier in his unit—a married man who had been on several lengthy deployments— told him that the less contact he had with his family, the less he would miss them and the easier it would be to get through the time apart. Scott had taken the more experienced soldier's advice seriously, which is why he had contacted her so infrequently. Kristina knew the man's wife, and told Scott how difficult the deployment had been for her.

"Do you know that during the entire deployment, that woman has heard from her husband only four or five times?" Kristina asked. "She tries to put on a brave face in public, but anyone can see how hurt she is. Just like you hurt me, Scott."

Scott nodded gravely.

"I need you to remember that you are the only one with the power to decide if and when we talk," she continued. "If I have a bad day and need your help or advice, I can't call you. I have to sit here and hope that you'll call me. All I do is wait. Can you imagine how bad that feels?

"If I've learned anything while you've been gone, it's that as much as it hurts to miss you, it hurts a lot worse to feel cut off. There are so many different feelings," she said, taking his hand, "and if I can't talk to you about them, then who can I talk to?"

"You're right," Scott said. "I'm sorry. I never meant to hurt you. I guess I just never thought about how any of this was affecting you. I was just thinking about what was easiest for me. But that's going to change. I promise. When I go back, I am going to call and email as much as I can. Things are going to be different, Kristina. I swear."

JUST END IT

Just as Kristina's marriage was coming back together, Diane's was on the brink of falling apart. On a snowy Sunday morning in late January, she sat fuming on the couch while her two sons argued over control of the television remote.

"Give it to your brother!" she said sharply to her older son, "You already had a turn. Do you need to go to your room?" The boys had been at it all morning, and she was at her wit's end. Not now, she thought. Not today. She desperately needed some time alone, some time to think. She had to decide if, and how, she was going to end her marriage.

Six days earlier Diane had come home from work and logged

on to the computer, as had become her habit, hoping that Thomas would be online. As a partial byproduct of his demotion, Thomas had been temporarily transferred to a new job in the tax center[1] and had regular access to email in the evenings. Since then it had become their routine to spend an hour or more chatting online every evening after work. That evening was no exception, and Thomas logged on shortly after she did. When they finished their lengthy conversation, Diane went into the joint email account that she and Thomas shared, looking for a friend's address. As she scanned the address book, a woman's name that she had never seen before caught her attention. She read the name over and over again, her heart rate surging with rage, not wanting to believe what she saw. The woman's address could mean only one thing: Thomas was meeting women online again.

Thomas's online relationships had been the biggest source of discord in their marriage for years. Diane had first stumbled upon Thomas's platonic but, from her perspective, no less offensive extramarital relationships several years earlier while they were at Fort Lewis, Washington. One morning she left for work with Thomas still at home on his day off, captivated as usual by the glowing computer screen. Halfway into her commute the car wheezed and sputtered to a stop, and Diane stomped to a pay phone to call Thomas for help. The phone line was busy, so she waited ten minutes and then called again. Still busy. It took almost two hours for her to get through. When she finally reached him, she demanded to know what he had been doing to tie up the phone line all that time. Thomas confessed that he had been on the Internet, visiting chat rooms, meeting other women online.

Diane was outraged. She couldn't stand the thought of her husband seeking out the company of other women, women with whom he was sharing intimate details of his life, of *their* life. It was a betrayal, and she wanted it to stop. Thomas begged for forgiveness and swore that he would stop visiting the chat rooms. For a while he did, but in a matter of weeks he was back on the computer, often spending hours a day chatting with strangers. Diane pleaded with him to go into marriage counseling with her and he agreed, but after only a few weeks of counseling, Thomas was sent on an eight-month deployment to Bosnia, and the unresolved issues were simply pushed aside.

Several years later, when they relocated to Baumholder, Diane and Thomas resumed counseling with another chaplain. The chaplain tried to impress upon Thomas how much his Internet activities were threatening his marriage and urged him to stop, but Thomas, despite his sincere efforts to improve other aspects of the marriage, simply could not understand why Diane had such a problem with his online relationships. He had grown up with sisters and was used to confiding in women, that was all. There was no sex, he insisted, just talking; surely there was no harm in that. Diane had hoped that in time Thomas would come to accept the chaplain's advice, but once again, only two months into counseling, Thomas deployed to Iraq.

Now, staring at evidence of Thomas's latest liaison, Diane was livid. He had promised her that he wasn't going to do this anymore, and she had been foolish enough to believe him.

She opened up a new window and typed in Thomas's address. "I know about her..." she wrote furiously. "Don't call me. Don't write to me. I want nothing further to do with you. It's over!"

Disregarding her unequivocal request, Thomas called her at work the following morning, and she agreed to meet him online later that evening. As he had done so many times before, Thomas begged for her understanding and forgiveness. The woman was just a friend, he said; there was no reason to feel threatened. But Diane did feel threatened. All she and Thomas had between them now was email, and his willingness to share that with another woman felt more like infidelity than any of his previous online dalliances. "Why don't you just end it?" she typed, seething with anger. "I'm already on my own. Just end it."

CHAPTER ELEVEN

Though separation from families has been the norm for soldiers and officers through history, the Information Age is giving troops the tools to stay in the picture. ... And unlike previous wars, soldiers in Iraq typically have some telephone contact, and more frequent mail and e-mail missives.
—Stars and Stripes[1]

STAIRWELL LIVING

Beth opened her eyes and looked out her bedroom window at another gray, snowy day. It would be a good day for sleeping in, she thought wistfully, not that she had that option. "I'm coming, Kathryn!" she yelled in response to her daughter's cries. She rolled out of bed, shrugged into a cardigan, and went to Kathryn's room to find out what was the matter.

"My horsie broke!" Kathryn wailed.

"Well that wouldn't have happened if you weren't so rough with it," Beth said patiently. "Here. Why don't you give it to me and let me see if I can fix it."

Beth took the horse, which was really a broom-like stick with some padded cloth in the shape of a horse's head on one end, and slid the head back on, securing it with a piece of string. "Here you go," she said. "All better now. But remember, you have to be gentle."

Kathryn grabbed for the toy gleefully, slid the handle between her knees, and galloped through the apartment, neighing at full volume. It's way too early for this, Beth thought as she shuffled to the kitchen to put on a pot of coffee.

"Kathryn! Come here, honey," she called. The little girl galloped in. "I'm going to make breakfast Do you want to pick out a video?"

Kathryn plopped down on the floor in front of a wide array of children's videos that Beth placed in front of her. Looking down at her daughter sorting through the pile of animated movies, Beth felt a twinge of guilt. If anyone had told her before she became a mother that she would let her child watch this much television, she would never have believed it. She had always looked down on parents who left their children planted in front of the television set instead of engaging them with books and educational activities. But the videos were the only way she could get Kathryn to sit still long enough to get anything done, and early in the deployment she had found herself relying on her "TV babysitter" far more than she would have liked.

Beth served breakfast and then, with Kathryn still absorbed in the world of Disney, went to the computer, checked the news—it was a good morning; no casualties so far—and opened up the Excel spreadsheet she was working on for the battalion. At a recent FRG meeting the battalion commander's wife had asked for help creating a new database of spouses that would be easier for FRG leaders to access and update. As one of the few people in the room with experience working with spreadsheets, Beth had volunteered. It was a far cry from the way she had once thought she would put her MBA to use, but at least the project required a modicum of thought and creativity, more than she could say for her average day. She had gotten through less than a page when the phone rang.

"Hi!" she said excitedly when she heard Doug's voice on the line. "Daddy's on the phone!" she stage whispered to Kathryn. Beth turned off the TV so that she could hear Doug better, and after a few minutes handed the phone off to Kathryn. Kathryn still didn't quite understand the concept of telephones and rarely said much to her father when he called, but Beth knew that her daughter liked hearing his voice. After a minute or two Kathryn gave the phone back and Beth reached for a car repair invoice she had been saving for Doug's call.

Beth knew that many other wives of deployed soldiers wouldn't have mentioned the invoice. They shielded their husbands from such banal aspects of domestic life and were convinced that even the slightest distraction from the home front would lower the soldier's alert level, which could have deadly consequences. Sick children, sprained ankles, fights between family members, bills, disappointment about missed birthdays and anniversaries, even expressions of fear and loneliness…all of it was off limits until the deployment was over. Beth wasn't prepared to cast judgment on any else's marriage, but for hers, she thought that kind of censorship was a mistake. Doug liked to know that he was still a necessary part of the family. Even in Baghdad, he still wanted to feel included. And she needed his input. She didn't feel right making significant financial decisions without his consent, and she certainly didn't want to leave him in the dark when she or Kathryn had a health problem or she was having a particularly bad day. She and Doug had always been extremely open with one another —she had always thought of that openness as one of the best parts of their marriage—and losing it would have been a strain on both of them. They were a family, and deployment or no deployment, she thought it was important to act like one.

As Beth started to explain the car's latest breakdown, Kathryn resumed playing with her horse, crawling under the dining room table and neighing at the top of her lungs. "Kathryn, shhh," Beth said. "I'm trying to talk to Daddy." Kathryn ignored her and the neighing continued at the same pitch.

"What in the world is that noise?" Doug asked.

"That noise is your daughter," Beth sighed. "See all the fun you've been missing?"

Later that afternoon, Beth helped Kathryn into her shoes and winter coat so that they could head over to a friend's apartment for a play date. They were halfway out the door when Beth heard her next door neighbor's door creak open. A man walked out and bounded down the stairs without pausing to make eye contact. By the time Beth and Kathryn got down the stairs he was gone, but two of her downstairs neighbors stood in the hallway, casting disapproving glances up the stairwell.

"There he goes again," one of the women said with a smirk.

"You'd think she'd try to hide it," the other retorted. "God. The nerve of her! There her husband is, getting shot at every day, and she's running around with another guy. Pisses me off."

Beth kept her own thoughts on the matter private. She had seen the guy coming and going from her neighbor's apartment for weeks, and each time she was left feeling less outraged than sad. She didn't know the woman well, but she did know that there had been a lot of problems in the marriage prior to the deployment. According to talk in the stairwell, the husband had been cheating before he left, and Beth could only assume that the woman's affair was, at least in part, payback. They were a young couple, with a baby less than one year old, and while Beth found her neighbor's actions reprehensible, her focus was more on the ramifications. Within a matter of months that woman's husband was going to return. Surely he would find out about the affair she had taken so few pains to hide, and what would happen to them then? What would happen to their baby? It was going to be bad for everyone.

Beth hurried out of the stairwell, hoping not to get sucked into the conversation. Whatever her neighbor was doing with that guy was none of her business. Beth wanted to stay as far away from the whole disappointing, seedy situation as possible.

LONG DISTANCE EITHER MAKES YOU
OR BREAKS YOU

Every day since Diane discovered Thomas's poorly concealed online relationship, he had sent a stream of apologetic emails, pleading with her to give him another chance. But Diane remained resolute. She had given him chance after chance and this time it was really over. "I've wiped the board clean so many times that it stays chalky," she wrote. "I'm ready to walk out."

She emailed friends back in the States, asking them to look into what kinds of jobs were available to someone with her limited qualifications. She knew the pickings were going be slim: She had joined the Coast Guard straight out of high school, stayed only long enough to get pregnant and enter into her disastrous first marriage, and had held only menial jobs since then. She had hoped to enroll in a free, dental hygienist training program that the Army offered while she was in Baumholder, but enrollment was restricted due to the program's immense popularity, and she had not been accepted. She didn't have a college degree, had no technical training, and because she and Thomas had moved around so often, had never been able to establish much of a work history. Still, she told herself, "It's in God's hands now. He will open a door." If she was supposed to leave Thomas and set out on her own with the boys, something would come up sooner or later.

It all would have been a lot easier if she could have relied on the support of her family, but Diane knew not to even consider that as an option. Years earlier, when her first marriage had collapsed and she had nowhere else to turn, her mother and stepfather had grudgingly taken her in, but they had made her feel so unwelcome that she fled at the earliest opportunity. She had never had anyone she could turn to when her life fell apart and that was part of the reason she had never left Thomas when things got bad between them; she had nowhere else to go. Making matters worse, there was no one in Baumholder she could turn to for support. The chaplain they had begun counseling with prior to the deployment had been sent to a different post months earlier, and she had no real friends locally in whom she could confide. She knew that if she were going to follow through on her threat to end her marriage, she would have to do it on her own.

Diane waited anxiously for news about the job and housing markets from her friends, while Thomas continued to barrage her with pleadings not to leave him. By the end of the week, he shifted to a different tactic, hoping that if they could not resolve the contentious issue, perhaps they could just ignore it.

"So, how was your week?" he asked hopefully.

"My week was terrible and you know very well why," she shot back.

"Yes," he said, undeterred by her hostility. "But how was it other than that?" He didn't get it. There was no separation between their fighting and the rest of her week. She was hurt and angry, and a few contrite emails were not going to solve the problem this time.

When that approach failed, Thomas shifted his tactics again, this time going on the attack. Jealousy had plagued their marriage from the start, and the long separations the military lifestyle imposed had only increased that tension. Ever since the beginning of the deployment, Thomas had been deeply suspicious of Diane, and often mentioned stories he had heard about infidelity back in Baumholder, insinuating that she might be doing the same.

Diane was well aware of Thomas's jealous tendencies, and had gone out of her way to allay his fears. Sure, she admitted, she looked at other men from time to time. She had longings, but she suppressed them. She avoided situations in which she might be tempted, steering clear of the local bars and nightclubs, and she never drank, wary that it could lower her inhibitions to the extent that she might do something she would regret. Instead, she came home from work, turned on the computer, and waited for Thomas to log on.

All throughout the deployment Diane had minimized even the most innocuous contact with men, concerned that even an innocent encounter could get back to Thomas, twisted through the vicious rumor mill into something illicit. Recently, when a male coworker invited her out to lunch, she cleared the invitation with Thomas before accepting. Thomas had raised no objection at the time, but now that his indiscretion had been uncovered he went on the offensive, suggesting that there had been more to the lunch than what she had described as two acquaintances from work chatting over fried chicken at the food court.

Diane was incensed at the accusation. "I don't see people!" she fired back. "I don't have a life!"

Diane could not believe he had the audacity to accuse her of cheating at a time like this. "If I were going to cheat, it would have happened when you were in Bosnia," she wrote, referring to a particularly difficult period in their marriage. "But I didn't then and I haven't now. You know, there is a bit of a double standard going on here. You can have relationships with other women online but I can't even go to lunch with a guy from work?"

God will open a door. That is what Diane said when she sent off emails to friends back in the States asking them to look into job opportunities for her. But when three weeks passed and not a single viable opportunity had presented itself, her resolve to walk away from her marriage weakened.

Diane's experience in the mailroom was not enough to qualify her for a job in the U.S. Postal Service, and none of the other jobs offered enough pay to support a single adult with two children. Apartment prices in her hometown of Austin, Texas, had sky-rocketed with the recent tech boom in that city, and all the jobs that paid a decent wage required a college degree and computer skills. Every day she checked her email, hoping to find an encouraging response from someone, but day after day all she got was disappointing news.

And so, as the weeks passed and Thomas continued to beg her to stay, she began to reconsider the decision to end her marriage. "I asked God to show me where to go and only one door opened," she said, "and Thomas was standing in it."

Thomas convinced her that this time, he really was going to make an effort to change. Every day after work they talked online, rehashing issues of trust and betrayal in their marriage, and although none of the conversations were new, this time they actually took the time to listen to each other. "Sometimes it takes something like this to get you to talk about this stuff," Diane explained. "Usually we just skim the surface."

Diane admitted to Thomas that she understood, at least in part, his fixation with the Internet. She was not interested in chat rooms, but she could easily spend hours, not to mention dollars, on eBay. She could see what an addictive medium the Internet was (she had often commented that if the computer had breasts, it would be Thomas's ideal companion) and she did not want to deny her husband the pleasure he got from it, especially while he was under so much stress, but she did not want that pleasure to come at the expense of their marriage either.

After hours of online discussion they reached a compromise. Diane conceded that if Thomas needed to deal with his loneliness in Iraq by going into chat rooms, she could accept that. What she could not accept was the sneaking around. "If it involves another human being, tell me," she told him. She didn't mind his having casual conversations with strangers, as long as she knew about them and as long as he wasn't sharing anything too personal. "Taking your intimate thoughts and feelings and giving them to another woman crosses the line," she warned.

This was the closest she had ever come to leaving Thomas, and even with the worst of the episode behind them, Diane still felt uneasy about what the future would hold. Each time there was a pause in their instant messaging sessions she wondered if he was talking to another woman, and she knew that it would be difficult, if not impossible, to ever fully trust him again. But for now, at least, she was determined to look beyond her suspicions and make the marriage work. "Every day we have to fight to keep it going," Diane said of her marriage. "Long distance either makes you or breaks you, and with us it nearly breaks us, then we pull it together again."

CHAPTER TWELVE

"We have somebody looking into the eye of every soldier and making sure they are okay."

—*Lt. Col. Todd A. Buchs,*
222ⁿᵈ Base Support Battalion commander,
announces plans for the reintegration of Baumholder's soldiers
back into the community, February 24, 2004

AN INKLING OF HOPE

At 9:30 on a brisk late February morning, a crowd of Baumholder spouses filed into the newly renovated Wagon Wheel movie theater for a town hall meeting. The meeting, which had been called to announce the redeployment home of First Armored Division soldiers within the next couple of months and to answer questions about what would happen once they returned, was one that people had anxiously anticipated since it had been announced. Spouses filled every seat and latecomers lined the aisles, juggling notepads, baby strollers, and bags of snacks.

Lieutenant Colonel Todd A. Buchs, the 222ⁿᵈ Base Support Battalion commander, took the microphone, introduced himself, and said, "We're here to answer your tough questions."

"When is my husband coming home?" muttered a young mother as she cradled an infant in one arm and restrained a toddler with the other.

As if in answer to her question, the commander went on, "The only question I can't answer is, 'When are they coming back?'" The audience broke into nervous laughter; that had become the million-dollar question, and everyone was hoping for an answer.

Colonel Buchs explained that as soon as the soldiers redeployed, they would go through a seven-day decompression period. Soldiers would spend part of their days away from their families, in-processing, going through medical examinations, completing financial paperwork, and attending a series of briefings on everything from dealing with spouses and family members to drinking responsibly to driving in Germany. The idea, he explained, was to give the soldiers a full week to adjust to being back at home in a controlled environment before they were turned loose on a month of block leave, 30 days of paid vacation that most soldiers would be granted upon the completion of their one-year combat tour. Everyone in Baumholder remembered the shocking killings of five Army spouses at Fort Bragg during the summer of 2002, after the return of soldiers from operations in Afghanistan, and the Army was doing everything possible to prevent any future incidents of redeployment-related violence.

That unsettling topic out of the way, the colonel went on to discuss what he knew was the most important day of the seven-day reintegration period to everyone in the room: Day Zero, the homecoming.

"Now I know you're not going to like this," he began, "but no spouses are going to be allowed to meet the soldiers at the airport."

Tasha, who was sitting in the balcony with several friends from her FRG, turned to the woman sitting next to her. "Oh no they didn't!" she said indignantly. The crowd around her echoed her disbelief with loud cries and boos of disapproval.

"I know. I know. But hear me out," the colonel continued patiently. "The soldiers have to turn in their equipment and go through a security clearance before they can be released and reunited with all of you, and we want to make that happen as quickly as possible. If we have spouses coming to the airport, all that's going to do is make the wait even longer."

Tasha kept her arms crossed defiantly in front of her chest, but sat back in her seat quietly and waited for the colonel to finish.

"Once all the soldiers in the company have been cleared, they will be sent as a unit to the gymnasium where, no matter what

time it is, there will be banners, patriotic music, and most importantly, you. We'll have a brief ceremony, then we'll drop the chain
and you guys can reintegrate."

The audience responded to the unintended innuendo with a
spontaneous thunder of applause, hoots, and whistles.

There was an end in sight, it seemed. Charlie Company 2-6,
which had deployed six weeks before most of Baumholder's troops,
was scheduled to return in mid-March, and while an actual return
date for the rest of Baumholder's companies remained frustratingly elusive, it was all but certain that they would be home by
the end of April. Gigantic tents went up in the movie theater
parking lot to house the reintegration training events, and Army
Community Services set up reunion trainings designed to teach
spouses to look for signs of emotional trauma in returning soldiers and to help families prepare for the adjustment of having a
soldier back at home again. Families who had gone back to the
States for the duration of the deployment returned to Germany,
excited spouses packed the on-post travel agency to make plans
for block leave, and welcome home banners and yellow ribbons
covered apartment building entrances and fences. Finally, it
seemed, the long, terrifying wait was almost over.

Almost over, but not quite. Soon after the meeting, still feeling hopeful about her husband's return, Beth started her day as
she always did by checking the Yahoo! news Web site, praying
that no soldiers had been killed in Iraq overnight. This time, like
so many times before, her prayers failed her. The headline read:
"Five Soldiers Killed in Iraq." Please God, she whispered, don't let
it be First Armored Division. Holding her breath, she clicked on
the link. The soldiers were from a different division; Doug was
still alive, or was to the best of her knowledge. She let out a sigh of
relief, thankful that it was no one she knew, but her relief was
immediately followed by guilt. The fallen soldiers might not have
been her husband or any of her neighbors' husbands, but they
were *someone's* husband, father, son, or brother. How terrible to
feel relief at their deaths! Yet as much as she detested it, the
relief was undeniable, and she felt it every time she read that an
attack had taken place not in Baghdad but in Mosel or Fallujah,

anywhere outside First Armored Division's control.

Beth couldn't imagine getting this far into a deployment, when she finally had an inkling of hope that the whole ordeal would soon be over, only to find that she had relaxed too soon. Her anxiety about Doug's safety never lessened its icy grasp. Even though he spent most of his time in a relatively safe desk job—far safer than many other soldiers in his company who regularly patrolled the streets of Baghdad on foot and in unarmored Humvees—she knew that there were still ample opportunities for danger. Just last weekend he had called and said that he only had a few minutes to talk because he was on his way to a classified destination and had to get out to the convoy. As soon as she hung up the phone, terrifying images of the convoy running over an IED (an improvised explosive device, also referred to as a roadside bomb) and Doug being blown to bits flooded her mind. All she could think of was the fact that if Doug died, the last time she would have held his hand or given him a kiss would have been months ago. How do you grieve for something like that? she wondered. If he were home and got into a lethal car accident, at least she would have seen him the night before, told him she loved him before he left the house. If he got killed now, she thought, it would almost be like mourning a ghost.

THE WRONG KIND OF HOMECOMING

On a dark, chilly evening Teresa gathered up a few bags of tortilla chips and an overnight case and drove to Buddy Night. The host for tonight's gathering was a woman named Kimberly, a petite, blond major's wife with a cheerleader-like disposition and a fondness for Americana. The hallway leading into her apartment was festively lit by sparkling tea light candles that set off red, white, and blue pottery, blankets, and old fashioned tins painted with American flags. Inside, the lights were dimmed, her well-kept apartment filled with Polish pottery, crystal displays, and framed family photographs.

The hostess poured glasses of wine and steered the new arrivals to the dining room table, which was already heavily laden with food, insisting that this time no one was going to spend the whole evening in the kitchen. As more guests arrived, even more food crowded the table—bean dip and chips, cream cheese roll ups, spinach pinwheels, ham and cheese croissants, donut holes, chocolate chip cookies, and other fat- and calorie-laden comfort food. Ushered into the dining room, the women gathered around the table, passing plates of food and refreshing wine glasses while they shared stories from the past week.

The battalion commander's wife commented that she was finally starting to see an end to the deployment. Soldiers from Charlie Company would be coming home in a matter of weeks, and even though her own husband wouldn't be among them, she was excited to see soldiers starting to return to post.

"Are you kidding?" another woman chimed in. "I saw the soldiers returning to Wiesbaden on TV and I lost it!"[1]

"Girl," Heather said, "just looking at that photo in the *Stars and Stripes* of the soldier hugging his wife and child got me all choked up."

"It feels like it is finally ending," Jennifer added. "I mean, I always knew it would end, but now it feels like it is really going to happen."

The other women in the room nodded their heads in agreement. There were still three months to go, but already the excitement was palpable; they were over the hump.

Reaching over a mound of guacamole for a cookie, Teresa began relating a story from the previous weekend. After Buddy Night, she had spent the night at a friend's house to avoid the drive back to her off-post apartment, and they were already in their pajamas and settling in for the evening when Nancy, the friend who had led the prayer on Thanksgiving, banged frantically on the front door, pleading for help. There was a vicious, rabid cat, she said, a huge one, in her building, and someone had to get it. "Hurry!" she pleaded. Teresa threw a trench coat on over her pink pajamas, and holding a mop like a machine gun she and her friend set off to save the post from the *Pet Cemetery*-like creature Nancy had described. As Teresa told it, the two pajama-clad women stalked the animal, disregarding their own safety in order to protect their friends and neighbors. Incredulous listeners repeatedly interrupted, asking, "Hang on. This was a cat, right? The 'meow, meow' kind?"

"Anyway…" she said, getting back to her story. They chased the ferocious creature through one building and into another, eventually trapping it on the top floor. Teresa boldly approached the animal and flipped on the light. And there, cowering in the corner, was not the rabid, dangerous beast she had been expecting, but a scared, hungry kitten that meowed plaintively as she approached, probably someone's pet who had accidentally been locked out while the family was away for R&R leave. The group howled with laughter as Nancy tried in vain to defend herself. "No, really," she insisted. "You didn't see this thing. It was really scary!"

Meanwhile, down at the other end of the table, Heather and Jennifer were reminiscing about a pottery-buying trip they had taken to Poland the previous year.[2]

"I couldn't believe it," Jennifer lamented. "There we were, surrounded by all this great, cheap stuff, and Rob wouldn't let me buy a single dish."

"He wouldn't let you?" the others asked in mock horror.

"Not one plate," Jennifer said. "He was in on the whole wedding registry so he knew what we had, and he seems to think we have enough plates."

The women groaned. You should never let your husband in on the registry, they said, and besides, everyone knew that there was no such thing as too many plates, especially when Poland was this close! They all agreed that they would have to make another trip, this time *without* Jennifer's husband.

The conversation turned to talk of vacations and romantic weekends once the soldiers came home, and Heather became atypically quiet. Her husband was supposed to be home by now. He had been scheduled to return to Baumholder that month so that they could move on to their next assignment, but just before he was due to leave, the stop-move/stop-loss policy came back into effect. Now he would have to finish out his tour with the rest of his company. Teresa, realizing the reason for her friend's long face, walked over and put her arm around Heather's shoulder. "You know," she teased, "As soon as I found out about stop loss I thought, Oh no, she is going to be crying out the window again. You should hear her cry." She imitated a loud, out of control wailing.

"Oh, and what about you?" Heather retorted, doing her own imitation of the high-pitched, squeaky cry that an injured mouse might make.

"I don't sound like that!" Teresa declared. Jennifer and Heather shot her a knowing look. "Okay, maybe a little," she admitted.

The evening went on that way for hours, friends teasing each other and laughing, overeating and promising to go the gym the next day, swearing that next time they would "be good" and knowing that come next Friday they would do the exact same thing all over again. Friday nights were something they had all come to look forward to; no matter how bad the week had been, they knew Friday night would offer some companionship and relief.

In the coming weeks and months the friends from Buddy Night would come to rely on one another more than they ever imagined. Before the deployment was through, one of these women would be visited by the dreaded soldiers in Class A uniforms. But that would be months later; for now, Teresa had a more immediate crisis to handle.

On a Saturday afternoon a couple weeks later, Teresa drove home from class, stopped briefly at Jennifer's apartment for a visit, then returned home to study for an exam she had coming up in her master's program. She threw down her bags and checked the answering machine to find a message waiting from her mother-in-law, asking her to return the call immediately. Teresa's father-in-law was in the emergency room. Doctors had found lesions on his brain, possibly cancerous.

Teresa was staggered by the news. She had just seen her father-in-law over Christmas and he had seemed fine then. What she didn't know yet was that Danny's father had been acting strangely for several weeks. He often spoke incoherently, lost his train of thought, and stared abjectly at once familiar objects as if he no longer recognized them. Assuming a long-dormant drinking problem had resurfaced, the family had avoided the unpleasant subject, and it was not until he went to visit his eldest son and daughter-in-law in Northern California that his medical condition was discovered. The couple was alarmed by his bizarre behavior and insisted that he go the emergency room to be examined. It was there that doctors first found the lesions and strongly recommended immediate treatment.

Teresa called Danny's brothers, hoping that one of them could give her more information. No one could, but one brother, the one who had taken his father to the emergency room, told Teresa that he thought that his father had known something was very wrong for weeks, but had been holding on for Danny's sake, hoping that without a diagnosis he could forestall the family crisis that he knew would take the greatest toll on his youngest son, so far from home.

Later that evening, Teresa asked her father-in-law what he wanted her to tell Danny. "Unless they are reading me my last rites, don't tell him," he told her unequivocally. He feared that if Danny knew about his condition, he might lose focus on what he was doing in Iraq, and that loss of focus could put Danny and the soldiers under his authority in even greater mortal danger. Teresa was noncommittal, certain that Danny would never forgive her for keeping this from him.

She agonized over the decision of how and when to alert Danny, ultimately deciding to wait until his father saw the doctor again later that day; that way she could give him the most current information. She hoped against all reason that the doctors might come back with a more positive prognosis, but deep down she knew that this was the beginning of the end. She called her mother for support, who listened compassionately, then reminded her gently that she had to be strong for her husband. Teresa knew what she had to do but wondered if she had the strength. She curled up in bed and sobbed.

She never slept that night. Finally, at 5 a.m., Danny's mother called. They had seen the doctor again and the news wasn't good. The tumor was cancerous; he could have several weeks to a few months to live, but there was no chance beyond that. All the other family members already knew; it was time to tell Danny.

Teresa called Kimberly, the woman who had hosted Buddy Night a few weeks earlier. As the battalion executive officer's wife, Kimberly had a direct phone link to her husband. She listened patiently as Teresa apologized for waking her at such an early hour and explained the situation in stops and starts. Teresa asked her to call her husband and get a message to Danny to call home as soon as possible, then gave her a list of people that Danny should have with him for emotional support. Probably no more than 20 minutes passed before Danny called, but the wait felt interminable.

"What's up?" Danny's voice asked through the receiver. He sounded rushed and slightly irritated. Teresa took a deep breath and explained, in her most matter-of-fact tone, what had happened, hoping to get through it without crying. Danny listened quietly until she had finished, then asked a few specific questions. What was the exact prognosis? When was his father going to see a specialist? Was the insurance going to cover his care?

Teresa answered his questions as best she could, and promised that as soon as she knew anything more, she would email him. "Are you okay?" she asked.

"I'm fine," he said curtly. "I have to go to a meeting now." He hung up before she could say goodbye.

Utterly exhausted, Teresa collapsed into a chair and told herself that the hardest part was done. She skipped her class on Sunday and barely managed to drag herself to work on Monday. She never stopped dwelling on the pain Danny must be feeling and desperately wished she could be by his side to help him. All she wanted to do was get on the next plane to Baghdad, but of course, that was out of the question.

Two days later Teresa's mother-in-law called again. Danny's father had taken a turn for the worse, and the doctor was recommending that all the children come home immediately. If Danny wanted to see his father alive again, he had to come home now. Teresa sent the Red Cross message downrange: *You need to come home. This could be it.*

Once the Red Cross message came through, the chain of command pushed through the red tape—his commanders had already

promised Danny that if his father's situation worsened, he could
leave immediately. They got Danny on a flight scheduled to depart for Germany later that evening. Before he left, the battalion
commander took Danny aside. He assured Danny that he had
done everything the unit needed him to do and that there were
too many lieutenants in the company anyway. Danny had become
redundant in Iraq, but he was needed at home with his family,
and family always had to come first. He also instructed Danny to
remember his wife and the fact that she had been waiting for him
for a long time. Pay attention to her needs as well as your own, the
colonel advised.

Back in Baumholder, Teresa spent the morning in a state of
shock, wandering around her apartment in her pajamas, unsure
what to do first. She had been living like she was back in college,
throwing her clothes on the floor and leaving dishes in the sink.
She couldn't remember the last time she had vacuumed or washed
the car, and there was virtually no food in the house. She couldn't
let Danny come home to this mess. I had two months to prepare
for this stuff, and now I have a day, she thought frantically. She
needed to clean the house, stock the refrigerator, pack, wash the
brand new BMW Danny hadn't even seen yet, prepare his Class
A uniform with all its ribbons and medals in case there was a
funeral, buy plane tickets, find a replacement for work...the list
went on and on; she could never do it in time.

She called Heather and Jennifer who came over immediately
to help answer the constantly ringing phone so that Teresa could
take a shower. Then the friends divided up her to-do list between
them.

"Don't worry about anything," Jennifer said reassuringly.
"We've got everything under control."

"This is just so hard," Teresa replied. She was on the verge of
seeing her husband after so many months apart, and she couldn't
even get excited. Their reunion was supposed to be a celebration,
but there was nothing to celebrate in Danny's coming home to
watch his father die.

Danny's flight was cancelled two days in a row. Finally, on
Friday, he called to tell her that he was flying out that night and

would get into Ramstein Air Base at 2:40 a.m. Desperate for distraction, Teresa drove to Buddy Night. As usual, the women were gathered around a feast of food and wine, and as soon as she arrived they jumped up to offer hugs and words of support.

"You know we love you," Kimberly said. "And even though we are sad about the reason, we are so glad that you and Danny are going to be together soon."

The other women seconded her remarks, while a few lightened the mood by teasing Teresa about the imminent return of her sex life.

Later that night Teresa drove to Ramstein, pulling into the airport parking lot at just before 2 a.m. She expected to be at least half an hour early, but as she approached the hanger, she saw a soldier in DCUs walking toward the car. She screeched to a halt in the middle of the parking lot and ran to meet him. "Hurry up and get back in the car," Danny yelled. "It's freakin' cold as shit out here!"

"Yeah," she said, smiling shyly. "It *is* cold." Shivering, they hugged and kissed, then scurried into the car to get warm.

Two days later Teresa and Danny left for California, hoping they would not be too late. Danny's father was still alive, but their first glimpse of him, lying weakly in a hospital bed, was devastating. He looked fragile and pale, his face appeared distorted, and he was only periodically lucid.

Danny walked up to his father's bedside, took a Marine Corps coin out of his pocket, and slipped it in his father's palm. Months ago, while Danny was working to rebuild an Iraqi hospital, Marine Corps General Peter Pace, the vice chairman of the Joint Chiefs of Staff, had visited the hospital as part of a tour of reconstruction projects in Baghdad. Danny delivered an impromptu briefing, and later mentioned that his father had been a Marine. General Pace retrieved a military coin from his pocket and told Danny to give it to his father the next time he saw him. Danny had carried the coin in his wallet ever since, looking forward to the day he could present it to his father in person; he knew how much it would mean to him. But when he handed his father the coin, no sign of recognition appeared on the proud former-Marine's face. It was then that Danny realized how far his father had deteriorated, and Teresa looked on helplessly as Danny's large blue eyes clouded with tears.

"Do you want me to leave you alone with your family for a while?" Teresa whispered.

Danny's grip around her waist tightened in reply. "I don't want you to be away from me," he said. "Ever."

SPRING

The top U.S. military officer said Thursday he could not estimate with confidence how long American forces will have to stay in Iraq.... For planning purposes, the Army is assuming it will have to keep roughly 100,000 troops in Iraq for at least another two years, other officials have said.

—Stars and Stripes[1]

CHAPTER THIRTEEN

Exactly a year and one day after departing for Iraq, Charlie Company, 2-6 Infantry Battalion is back in Baumholder. Charlie Company was the first large contingent of soldiers to depart for Iraq in March of last year and they are the first large group to return.

—Herald Union[1]

CHARLIE COMES HOME

On the afternoon of March 18th, excited women and children gathered on the basketball courts of the Hall of Champions. From inside the weight room next door, exercisers could hear patriotic music booming from loudspeakers that had been placed on either side of the bleachers. Suddenly the music stopped and a man took the microphone, announcing the long-awaited return of soldiers from Charlie Company 2-6. Several of the women in the weight room jumped off their StairMasters and sprinted to the doorway just in time to see the first soldiers march into the gymnasium as their ecstatic wives and children waived welcome home signs and cheered. The onlookers observed the joyful scene for several minutes, some smiling, others using their gym towels to wipe away tears.

"Finally!" one said.

"It's good to see them coming home," another agreed.

"Yeah, now I just want *my* husband to get here!" a third exclaimed.

The three women resumed their workouts, counting down the weeks until their own husbands would be marching through that door.

Soon after the return of Charlie Company, Jena also returned to Baumholder. She had unexpectedly spent the last two and a half months in Alabama, taking care of her terminally ill grandmother. Jena had always been extremely close to her grandmother, and it hurt her to see the woman she revered in such a debilitated, painful condition. Normally, she thought, a wife could turn to her husband for comfort as she helplessly watched a beloved grandparent creep toward death. Jena wished more than ever before that Adam could be by her side, but as much as she longed for his support, she kept her concerns to herself during their once-a-week phone calls; the last thing Adam needed was stress from home, and whenever he was able to call she made sure she sounded upbeat and positive so that he never had a reason to worry about her.

Each time the phone rang and it was Adam calling from Iraq, Jena's grandmother would shake her head in wonderment. She had been a young Army wife during World War II, and the amount of contact that Jena and Adam were able to maintain never ceased to amaze her. In her day, she told Jena during their long afternoon talks, the only communication she'd had with her husband while he was off at war was the letters that were often at least three months out of date by the time they arrived, if they arrived at all.

"You're very fortunate, Jena," her grandmother told her.

She was right, Jena thought. People in Baumholder did a lot of complaining about the length of the deployment, the danger, the hardship on the families, but when she compared her experiences to those of her grandmother's generation, every complaint paled in comparison. A lot of women in that generation had waited two and three times as long for their loved ones to return from war, and they had done so without the benefit of CNN, satellite phones, and email. We've gone soft, Jena thought, as she considered the sacrifices women had made throughout the ages during times of war. Comforted by the thought of all those generations of women who had gotten through far worse than what she was experiencing now, she felt a renewed sense of determination to endure the remaining weeks of the deployment with courage and grace.

That determination was buoyed the following week when Jena visited a fourth grade class at the local elementary school that had "adopted" Adam at the start of the deployment. The children sent Adam letters and drawings and an occasional care package; that much Jena knew. What she didn't know, prior to her visit, was that Adam had somehow found the time to write to each child in the class individually. Jena was shocked to find photos and letters from her husband posted on every wall in the classroom. Seeing those letters filled Jena with pride. It was just like Adam to do something like that so humbly, not even telling her about it. More importantly, knowing that he had come in from potentially deadly patrols, removed his weapon, and sat down to write letters to school children reassured her that he had not been overly affected by what he had seen and done in Iraq. The deployment might have changed him in some ways, but fundamentally, he was still the same kind, caring person he had always been. She drove back to her grandmother's house and told her all about the visit. "The soft part in him hasn't been interrupted," she concluded with a smile.

Jena cherished the time with her grandmother, no matter how emotionally draining, but she also missed the military community in Baumholder. Every few days she called her best friend in Baumholder to get caught up on the latest news and gossip. The two friends often joked that they had become more like a married couple than friends, filling in all of the roles that a husband or wife would play except for one. During one phone call, as they talked about the homecoming that now seemed right around the corner, Jena laughed that she had been on her own so long that she was almost nervous about having a husband around again. Jena's aunt overheard the conversation and shot her a disapproving glance.

"Jena!" the aunt scolded as soon as she was off the phone. "You shouldn't even joke about that sort of thing."

Jena tried to explain what she had meant. Of course she wanted to have Adam back—there was nothing she wanted more—but he had been gone a long time and she had gotten used to being on her own. Adjusting to a less independent lifestyle was going to

take some getting used to. But as Jena started to explain, she realized the futility of the discussion. She wouldn't have had to explain herself in Baumholder; everyone would have understood
immediately. Back home in Alabama, on the other hand, she knew
women who considered themselves abandoned when a husband
left on a weeklong business trip; outsiders to the military just didn't
get it.

As the weeks passed, her grandmother weakened to the point
that Jena could no longer care for her. Other relatives helped out
until suitable hospice care was found. Jena returned to
Baumholder, trying to make up for lost time. She went to the gym
daily, hoping to shed some of the extra pounds she had put on
during her time in Alabama. One of the items on her to-do list
had been to slim down a bit and she had made progress in the
early days of the deployment. But when cancer caused her grandmother to lose weight rapidly, Jena cooked only the most high-
calorie, starch-laden foods she could find. She scoured grocery
store shelves looking for foods that packed a calorie wallop, turning them into hearty, appetizing meals that she hoped would tempt
her grandmother into taking a few extra bites, but often Jena found
that she was the only one eating. Instead of losing weight as she
had planned, she soon noticed her clothes getting snug. Now that
she was back in a more normal routine, she wanted to use the few
remaining weeks before Adam came home to make up for the
indulgences that had lodged themselves on her thighs during the
past couple of months.

Apart from the gym, she spent most of her time preparing to
welcome the single soldiers in Adam's company back to
Baumholder. Her mother had convinced a local store to donate
take-out boxes decorated with American flags, and Jena and her
friends from the FRG cooked daily to fill them with homemade
cakes, breads, and dinners that they stocked in the barracks' freez-
ers. She wanted to make sure that every soldier—married or
single—returned to a home-cooked meal. She spent hours at the
barracks, washing bed linens, making up beds, and decorating
the hallways. And of course, there were countless preparations to
make for her own husband's return: meals to cook and freeze in

advance, a house to clean, his Class A uniform to prepare for his sister's wedding that May. She was so busy, in fact, that it sometimes seemed like the guys were coming back too soon.

SOON

On one of the first sunny days of spring, Kristina sat outside on her balcony, enjoying the sunshine warming her bare arms as she talked on the phone with Scott.

"I heard something about you," Scott said suggestively.

"Oh really," Kristina said, playing along. "What did you hear?"

"I heard you had a guy over last weekend," Scott replied in an inscrutable tone.

"What?" she shouted, bolting upright in alarm. "Scott, that's ridiculous! You know the only person here last weekend was my 14-year-old brother!"

"I know, I know," Scott laughed. "I talked to him while he was there, remember? Don't worry; I know nothing was going on."

"Who told you that?" Kristina demanded.

"One of the guys in my platoon heard it from his wife who, I guess, heard it from someone in the building," Scott replied. "Looks like someone has been spying on you."

Kristina was incensed. Although she adored her relatively spacious, sunny apartment, she hated the prying eyes of her neighbors; it was like living in a fish bowl. She had to watch every little thing she said and did, always wondering if something as innocent as a visit from her barely-out-of-puberty brother would prompt rumors of infidelity or if Child Protective Services would be called because she swiped Marie's bottom for running out into traffic in front of the PX.

"Seriously, Kristina, don't let it bother you. I shouldn't have brought it up," Scott said. "Listen, I've got to get going. Are you gonna be online later tonight?"

"Yeah," Kristina answered. "I'm supposed to have an FRG meeting later tonight but I don't think I'm gonna go."

"Okay, then," Scott said. "Unless we get stuck doin' something, I'll talk to you tonight."

"Okay. Talk to you tonight." Kristina confirmed. "I love you. Be safe."

"I will. I love you, too, babe" Scott said.

Gone were the days of waiting seven weeks for a phone call and hoping for a letter that never came; Scott had been true to his promise to contact Kristina more regularly once he returned to Iraq. He called or emailed every day that he was not out on a mission, and they had both purchased web cams so Marie and Tyler could participate in the conversations. Kristina and Scott shared everything in the weeks following R & R from the most insignificant details of their days to emotional confessions about how much they missed each other. Scott told her that in some ways the advice the older soldier had given him had been correct: He missed her a lot more now than he had before, when they'd had such little contact. Kristina understood; she missed him more too, and it hurt, but she wasn't sure that was such a bad thing. "The hardest part is that I miss my husband," she explained, but went on, "In a way I enjoy missing him. I don't feel as lonely."

As Kristina and Scott said goodbye, Marie, who had dressed herself that morning in a track suit and tennis shoes worn on the wrong feet, was busy with a spring cleaning project of her own invention, scrubbing the bars of the balcony gate with baby wipes. Marie had found out that her father was supposed to come home within weeks and her spring cleaning project was her way of helping her mother get ready.

Kristina had not wanted to tell Marie that Scott was coming home just yet. The homecoming was still weeks away and the date remained uncertain. But as they were driving through post the previous week, Marie had noticed the welcome home signs covering the fences and apartment buildings.

"Mama?" she had asked, pointing at one brightly colored bed sheet. "What does that say?"

Kristina had reluctantly read her the welcome home message, and ever since Marie had excitedly announced to every stranger she encountered, "My daddy is coming home!"

As excited as Marie was at the thought of her father coming home, Kristina could tell that the constant anticipation was hard on her. Kristina had no idea what "soon" meant to a three year old, and she and Scott worried that they had promised her that he would be home "soon" so many times that she would stop believing it. In fact, Marie had recently said something startling. She was talking about her cousin in Texas, and asked Kristina if her uncle was the little girl's father.

"That's right," Kristina told her. "He's her daddy."

Marie looked down and said in a sulky voice, "I don't have a daddy."

"Of course you do!" Kristina told her, explaining again that just because her daddy wasn't home didn't mean that she didn't have one.

Marie nodded and seemed to understand, but then said plaintively, "But he's gone."

Kristina did the only thing she could do. She bundled Marie up in her arms and held her tight, hoping that a mother's love would be enough to fill the void left by Scott's continuing absence.

After she hung up the phone, Kristina wandered around the apartment, wondering what to do next. This whole year she had wished time would move faster, but suddenly it was flying. She had been so busy the past couple of weeks that she had barely had time to pick up the kids' toys, much less do a thorough housecleaning. She'd had several visitors in the past few weeks—both of her brothers and friends from her hometown—and she had been so tied up with company that she still had not finalized their travel plans for block leave. She wanted to wash and iron all of Scott's clothes again so that they would be fresh for him, she had to choose outfits for her and the kids to wear for his homecoming ceremony, and she still had to figure out what in the world she was going to write on his welcome home banners. She wanted to come up with something original, something other than the *Welcome Home, Honey! We Missed You!* and *You're Our Hero!* signs she saw all over post, but what else was there to write?

Kristina decided that her next task should be selecting an outfit for Scott's arrival. She still had weeks to choose, but after her unkempt appearance when Scott returned for R&R, this time she wanted to be ready. Scott liked her in dresses, but she wasn't comfortable in them and anticipated having to wait for a long time at the ceremony. Better to choose a nice pair of pants and a shirt, she thought, something sexy but also comfortable. She rarely allowed herself to indulge in fantasies about their reunion, knowing how dangerous starry-eyed expectations could be, but as she flipped through hangers in her closet she let her mind wander and imagined the romantic dinner at home she would share with her husband once the kids were in bed. Soon, she told herself. He'll be home soon.

THE ONLY ONE

All over post spouses busied themselves with last minute projects in anticipation of the homecoming: crash dieting, spring cleaning, finalizing plans for block leave, tying yellow ribbons to every signpost and tree, filling hallways and fences with welcome home signs, and sprucing up the barracks for single soldiers. Everyone Diane talked to was bubbling over with excitement about seeing their husbands again soon. She wished she could share in their enthusiasm, but listening to all the talk of vacation plans and dreams of romantic reunions left her feeling alienated. She felt like the only woman in Baumholder who had mixed feelings about her husband's return.

She, too, had fantasies about Thomas's homecoming, but hers were a far more chilling version than those she heard from the eager wives in her FRG. In a recurring dream that she began having soon after soldiers from Charlie Company returned, Thomas stepped onto a plane leaving Baghdad, finally on his way home. But just as he settled into his seat for take off, the plane exploded into an angry ball of red and orange flames. Everyone aboard, including Thomas, was killed instantly.

She had the dream every few days now, and it was the same every time; Thomas was on his way home and then, suddenly, he was gone. She tried to make sense of it, and thought that it must have come from news of a plane that was shot down several months ago, killing a group of soldiers on their way home for R&R. Thomas was not out of harm's way yet, and she still feared for his safety; that was one explanation. But she suspected that there was another, darker reason behind the haunting dream. Part of her, a part she struggled to silence, thought that it might not be such a bad thing if Thomas never came back from Iraq. That way, she would never have to confront him, she would never have to make the agonizing decision of whether or not to keep fighting for a marriage that was often the source of so much conflict and pain; it would all be settled for her. "I don't wish him to be dead," Diane explained. "I just wish I knew which way to go."

Thomas's homecoming meant that they would be forced to confront all the problems they had tried to ignore during the deployment. "We had a lot of issues that have been put on the back burner for a whole year, and now he's coming back and everything's supposed to be hunky dory, but it won't be. All of those issues are still there," Diane said. "I miss him, but I don't miss all the crap that's gonna come back with him.... It's going to be rough when he comes home."

In the time Thomas had been gone, Diane had made an unsettling discovery about her marriage. Having her husband home, she found, made very little difference in her life. Whether Thomas was home or not, she was the one who took care of the finances, did all the housework, prepared the meals, and raised the children; none of that had changed during the deployment. Certainly he made a financial contribution, but given time to establish herself somewhere, perhaps she could find a job that could support her and the boys. She missed his companionship, but other than that, she could think of little else that he contributed, and after so many months without him that companionship was starting to seem less and less vital.

Thomas's expectations about their reunion only exacerbated Diane's anxiety. He often told her that he fantasized about them having nonstop sex in his first few weeks at home, a fantasy that Diane knew was not going to happen. With two children at home, they would have neither the time nor the privacy for such hedonism. Even their first night together was likely to be disappointing. She knew Thomas was hoping for an erotic welcome, but she thought that the more likely scenario was that his flight would get in late at night, she would arrive to pick him up with two sleepy children, and they would all go home and fall into an exhausted sleep. It wasn't romantic, but it was far more probable than what Thomas was imagining, and Diane feared that they were setting themselves up for a disastrous reunion.

Maybe, she thought sadly, she would be better off if Thomas never came home at all. It was impossible to predict what the coming months would bring or if their marriage would even survive what was bound to be a tumultuous reunion. All Diane knew for sure was that she was not ready for him to come home.

CHAPTER FOURTEEN

Troops from the 1ˢᵗ Armored Division are a likely choice should military officials extend tours to quell violence in Iraq, according to its division commander.

"With our experience and proven performance, we are probably the coalition's best option," [Major General Martin] Dempsey said. "Moreover, the division's soldiers and their families have invested too much, made too many personal sacrifices in support of this mission, to see it risked at such a critical time."

—Stars and Stripes[1]

BE CAREFUL WHAT YOU WISH FOR

On a Wednesday night in early April, Teresa and Danny worked in opposite sides of their apartment, picking up clothes and washing dirty dishes, not speaking as they passed one another in the hall. They had been back in Baumholder for less than two weeks, but the tension between them had already become unbearable. As the increasingly hostile days passed, Teresa found herself wishing for the unimaginable: that Danny would go back to Iraq.

Teresa and Danny had returned from California after two weeks. There had been no way of knowing how much longer Danny's father would live and they both had responsibilities back in Baumholder, so they had reluctantly decided to return to Germany with the cruel knowledge that their next trip home would be for a funeral.

At first, they were relieved to be back in Baumholder, away from the tragic vigil in California, but soon the stress of Danny's unexpectedly early return began to drive a wedge between the couple. Danny hated being home without the rest of his company and often told Teresa that he wished he could return to Iraq.

Against Danny's wishes, his commander had decided that, with the division scheduled to redeploy home within the next month, it was senseless for him to return. Instead, Danny was temporarily assigned to the rear detachment while he awaited the return of his fellow soldiers. He worried about them constantly, overwhelmed by the guilty feeling that he had shirked his responsibilities both as a soldier and a son, that people needed him both in Iraq and California and he was there for none of them. Instead, he spun his wheels doing busy work while his peers were in Iraq and his father lay dying in a hospital bed thousands of miles away.

Meanwhile, Teresa was struggling to strike a precarious balance between her role as a wife and all the other roles she had taken on. She had not realized how integrated into the community she had become while Danny was away, nor how many people relied on her for support. She was uncomfortable that her own husband was home—even if it was for such an unenviable reason—while her friends' husbands remained in danger. Even though she knew that Danny was supposed to be her first priority, she felt she could not abandon her friends and responsibilities simply because he was home. She had Buddy Nights to attend, friends to check in on, volunteer work for the FRG, homework to complete, her job, and none of it included her husband. She had longed for Danny to come home every day that he had been away, but now that he was back his presence almost felt like an intrusion.

The mutual guilt they felt about Danny being home while other soldiers were still deployed made the stressful reunion even more difficult. They sneaked around post, almost as if they were lovers engaged in an illicit tryst instead of a married couple. Teresa was careful to say as little as possible about Danny's homecoming to her coworkers at the Education Center. They never held hands or kissed on post, and they even split up at the commissary to avoid flaunting their reunion in front of women who still longed for their husbands to return.

One afternoon Teresa and Danny stopped by the community mailroom, walking as they always did with a few feet between them, when they ran into Tasha. Teresa and Tasha knew each other from the FRG, though their relationship had never extended beyond a brief exchange of hellos. Teresa had been put off by some of Tasha's bitter comments at FRG meetings, and Tasha was leery of officer's wives, who often struck her as snooty. Even though Teresa had always seemed friendlier and more down to earth than most, Tasha still kept her distance.

As Teresa and Danny approached Tasha stared openly. "What's *he* doin' home?" she asked resentfully.

"Family emergency," Teresa replied tersely. She hated this. Everyone assumed that they had gotten some kind of privilege, when in fact that couldn't have been farther from the truth. Teresa doubted that, if Tasha knew the circumstances, she would still have thought they had it so great. No one wanted her husband to come home to see his father on his deathbed, and the weeks after the grim vigil in California hadn't exactly been a picnic either.

Danny resented the amount of time Teresa spent away from him and complained that she was either with her friends or on the phone with them. He felt shut out of her life, which was suddenly full of new people and commitments. He lashed out at her, accusing her of being lazy and allowing the apartment to turn into a pigsty. Danny's jovial nature, which usually kept minor disagreements from blowing up into major battles, was no match for the immense stress that he and Teresa were under. They bickered constantly, and rarely did two days pass without a major fight, the worst of which blew up one morning in early April.

Ignoring Danny's objections, Teresa had agreed to host a scrapbooking party for the FRG that Friday night. Tension between them ran high, but they managed to reach an uneasy truce and spent Wednesday evening silently working to make the apartment suitable for company, each avoiding whatever room the other was in. Danny straightened up the living room while Teresa cleaned the bathroom, storing away Danny's shaving kit and anything else that wasn't aesthetically pleasing in the medicine cabinet. The next morning Danny went into the bathroom to shave. Teresa heard doors being opened and slammed shut, then Danny yelling, "Where is my razor? Where the fuck is my razor? Teresa! Where the FUCK is my razor?"

Teresa stormed into the bathroom, threw open the medicine

cabinet, and thrust the razor at him, livid that he had broken the promise he had made for Lent to stop the nonstop swearing he had brought back with him from Baghdad. "If you want to break your promises to me, that is one thing, but you don't break your promise to God!" she yelled. Danny yelled back, hurling insults and accusations, and Teresa responded in kind. "I hope you deploy!" she screamed. "I hope you go back to Falluja or wherever the rest of your unit is, because clearly that's where you want to be!"

"I want to go back," Danny responded angrily. "I certainly don't want to deal with you!"

With that last, poisonous exchange, they both left for work. Teresa tried to focus on the mountain of paperwork heaped on her desk, but she was hopelessly distracted. She was still fuming later that afternoon when Heather and Jennifer came into her office, their faces streaked with tears. They had just gone to the barracks to decorate for a homecoming ceremony that was expected to take place the following week, but when they arrived the door was locked. Taped to it was a note that read "Welcome home activities postponed until further notice."

In the past few weeks, as areas of Iraq threatened to erupt into renewed fighting, there had been rumblings about additional troop requirements and possible extensions, but no one had believed that First Armored Division soldiers, who were within weeks of completing their one-year tour, would be extended. Many soldiers had already set off for the safety of Kuwait, many more were already on the way, and everyone was certain that the deployment was finally all but over. But, as Heather and Jennifer stood outside the empty barracks staring at the note, they realized that the delay could mean only one thing: There was going to be an extension. Their husbands weren't coming home after all.

The three tearful women hugged each other and cried, and Teresa guiltily confessed that she and Danny had fought that morning, and in the heat of the moment she had told him to go back to Iraq. "Oh Teresa, what were you thinking?" Jennifer asked.

"I know, I know," Teresa said regretfully, wishing she could take back the words that now seemed like a curse.

Minutes later Danny walked in, his head hung low. He started to say something to Teresa but stopped himself and instead turned to focus his attention on all three women. Troops from Baumholder had been extended in Iraq, he said somberly, possibly for as long as four months. He would return to his unit in a couple weeks, as soon as he could get a flight out. Teresa stared at the floor and nodded. "That's good," she said in a trance-like voice. "They need you. You're rested and they need people who are rested."

"Are you okay?" Danny asked once Heather and Jennifer had left.

"Yes," she told him, her voice wavering. "Are you?"

He told her he was and then said tenderly, "I think that next time I come home, we should do a better job of getting back together."

A BAD DAY IN BAUMHOLDER

Meanwhile, Beth hung up the phone and staggered back against the dining room wall, unable to support her own weight. Breathe, she commanded herself, you have to breathe. Sobbing hysterically, she dialed her mother's number in Michigan. There was no answer. She dialed again, this time leaving a message. "Pick up! I need you!" she wailed, gasping for air.

Kathryn, who was terrified to see her mother so distraught, yelled in the background, "Pick up! My mommy needs you!" then turned to Beth and said in a small, scared voice, "Mommy, you're scaring me."

Beth dialed a third time and this time her mother, who was just returning from the grocery store, picked up the phone. Upon hearing her daughter's obvious distress, she assumed that Beth was calling to tell her that Doug had been killed, and she too began to cry. "I'm sorry," Beth sobbed into the receiver, collapsing on the floor. For minutes, that was all she was able to say.

Beth had first heard about a possible extension earlier that day, when a friend called to tell her about a rumor that soldiers from the First Armored Division were going to have to stay in

Iraq for several more months. Rumors had circulated through post over the past few days as news filtered out from the Department of Defense that additional soldiers might be needed to quell uprisings in Sadr City and elsewhere, but Beth had paid little attention to them. Rumors were always being spread in Baumholder, and most of them proved to be nothing but idle speculation. So when her friend called to tell her what she had heard, Beth replied that she simply didn't believe it. Only a few days ago the battalion commander's wife had given out actual return dates. Some soldiers were already on the way home, and even the last-to-leave follow-on parties were supposed to be home by mid-May. They had discussed plans for the homecoming ceremonies and everyone had been so happy; surely they couldn't stop the soldiers from coming home now.

Minutes later, Beth's friend called again. This time she was certain. Her FRG leader had just called to inform her that soldiers from Baumholder had been extended for up to 120 days. Beth hung up the phone abruptly and called her own FRG leader, Patty Johnson, the same woman who had cared for her after her operation last summer. Patty told her that she didn't know anything for sure, but that an emergency meeting had just been called. Oh my God, Beth thought. It's true.

Beth managed to pull herself together in time to get Kathryn to preschool that afternoon, but her composure was shaky. She hoped she would not run into anyone she knew, fearing that someone might notice her swollen face and ask her what was wrong, which she knew would set her off again. Sure enough, as soon as she exited her apartment she ran into a neighbor. "Did something happen?" the neighbor asked. The tears returned quickly and she barely managed to choke out news of the extension. The neighbor shook her head sadly and told Beth about a conversation she had recently overheard between a newly returned soldier and his wife. "A lot of boys from Baumholder are going to die," the soldier had said. Ever since then, the neighbor told Beth, she had known something awful was going to happen.

Beth's hands shook uncontrollably as she drove, and even though she had stopped her tears by the time she escorted Kathryn into the building, the school director saw her distress immediately. "I see you've heard," she said sympathetically. All the mothers coming into the preschool had heard, and as the women came in holding the hands of their uncomprehending, energetic three- and four-year-olds, each wore the same shell-shocked expression.

That evening Beth dressed Kathryn in her new spring dress—a short, sleeveless tunic with green trim—despite the rainstorm brewing outside. It was the dress Beth had picked out for Kathryn to wear for Doug's homecoming, and it had quickly become the little girl's favorite. Beth pulled Kathryn's arms into a bright pink cardigan for warmth, and promised her that if she was very good and stayed very quiet during the emergency FRG meeting, she would give her a present. Beth was prepared to offer any bribe necessary for good behavior; she was too emotionally drained to deal with anything else.

They parked on a side street near the chapel and hurried through the windswept rain to the entrance. Beth made her way to the front of the chapel and looked around for familiar faces. Soldiers from the rear detachment lined the outer aisles, while spouses and children filed into the seating area in silence. Most were young women, red faced and teary eyed, holding a young child or two. Many sat in groups of twos and threes, holding hands and sharing tissues as quiet tears slid down their cheeks and dropped onto the collars of their raincoats. Beth chose a seat in the second pew, far away from people she recognized from the FRG; she didn't want companionship right now, she just wanted to get this over with.

Captain Bromenshenkel, the rear detachment commander for the battalion, stood at the pulpit looking down. In his late twenties, with closely cropped red hair and wire-rimmed glasses, he was well liked by spouses in the battalion and known for his cheerful personality and relaxed manner. But this time his ready smile was absent, and as he looked up to survey the room he inhaled deeply. He cleared his throat and got straight to the point, announcing that the decision had been made to extend the First Armored Division for up to 120 days. The soldiers who were already waiting for planes in Kuwait would return to their units;

soldiers from Charlie Company would probably be called in from block leave and sent back to Iraq as well. All reunion ceremonies had been cancelled.

The announcement was met with silence; the only sounds were a few stifled sobs and rifling around in purses for clean tissues. Captain Bromenshenkel continued, commending the strength of the Baumholder community and the high morale down in Baghdad. Yeah right, Beth thought. Don't tell me to be strong, and please don't tell me that morale is high. We all know better than that.

She tuned out the rest of the captain's comments as her thoughts strayed to what the extension would mean for her family: no happy reunion, no family vacation, another missed birthday, another missed anniversary, another few months of what had become her daily reality of waking up each morning to wonder if her daughter still had a father. Worse still, she couldn't escape the feeling that they were tempting fate. There had been few casualties from Baumholder so far, but as she recalled the words repeated to her by her neighbor—"A lot of boys from Baumholder are going to die"—she couldn't help but think that adding on another four months seemed like they were pushing their luck.

BOXES

Earlier that week, Kristina had opened up the latest mangled box Scott had sent home from Iraq in preparation for his return. Every few days another box arrived, covered in green Army duct tape and looking like it had been through a sand storm. Kristina sorted through the extra towels and t-shirts, books, and mementos, and then dropped off the box carcasses at the on-post recycling center. She had hoarded boxes for months, always on the lookout for anything she could use to send Scott more freshly laundered t-shirts and cigarettes, but now there was no need. Scott was coming home; her days of box hoarding were over.

That Wednesday night, after she put the kids to bed, Kristina stayed up late to catch the 11 p.m. news. As she watched footage of soldiers and Marines digging in around Falluja, getting ready for battle, she silently prayed for their safe return, then shut off the TV and went to bed. She slept soundly that night, thankful that her own husband would be out of danger soon. Her sense of security was short-lived.

Early the next morning a friend called to ask if she had seen the morning news. CNN was reporting that the Department of Defense was considering extending troops who had already been in Iraq for one year. Kristina raced to the Internet to find out more, and was just opening up Yahoo! when the phone rang again. It was Scott, calling from Baghdad.

"What's going on there?" she asked breathlessly. "Do you have any news?"

Scott had no idea what she was talking about. He hadn't heard a thing except that there was going to be a briefing later on that day, and he assumed it was to discuss plans for moving out to the port in Kuwait. "I'll call you after the briefing and let you know when I'm getting out of here," he said confidently, and Kristina hung up the phone feeling tremendously relieved.

But several hours later she got word that an emergency FRG meeting had been scheduled for that evening. She could imagine only two possible reasons for the meeting; either there had been a large number of casualties from Baumholder—a scenario too horrible to contemplate—or the soldiers had been extended. It had to be the latter. Kristina burst into tears, crying harder than she had ever cried during the previous eleven and a half months of deployment. Her sadness quickly turned to rage and, unable to control her fury, she kicked the furniture and screamed. For two hours she let herself sob. She didn't want to be comforted or distracted; she wanted to cry until the pain was out.

Scott called that evening to tell Kristina what she already knew. The briefing had not been about the trip to Kuwait; it had been about the extension. "Man, that is not cool," he said incredulously. They had been so close; he just couldn't believe it. Now he would have to endure four more months of escalating violence and another brutal Iraqi summer.

"Well, at least we'll be getting another extra thousand dollars in the bank every month," he said, referring to the bonus the Army would pay to soldiers serving in a combat zone longer than 365 days.

"Between having my husband back and an extra four thousand dollars, I'll take my husband," Kristina said sullenly.

"I know, babe," Scott said. "I was just trying to find something positive in this."

Later that evening Kristina tried to explain to Marie that her father was not coming home in a couple of weeks as they had promised he would. "Marie," she said lovingly, "Daddy can't come home yet." Marie stared up at the ceiling, refusing to make eye contact, and said, "Uh huh. I want to watch my Strawberry Shortcake video." Kristina tried again, but Marie wouldn't listen. Kristina gave up and put on the video.

The next morning she woke up with a sense of dread. Somebody shoot me, she thought. Shoot me, or at least put me to sleep for the next four months. She was utterly exhausted, sick of having so little control over her life, of having no choice but to hang in there and keep getting through one day at a time until Scott came home. She went out to her balcony to smoke a cigarette and noticed the welcome home signs she had put up two days ago in anticipation of Scott's imminent return. There were yellow ribbons everywhere, an American flag, and two heart-shaped posters that Marie had designed. She couldn't bear to look at them, and with tears welling up in her eyes she began ripping them down. Just then, Marie wandered outside, observing her with a stunned expression. "Mama, why are you taking those down?" she asked. For the second time, Kristina tried to tell Marie about the extension, and this time the little girl listened, nodding as Kristina explained to her that it wasn't that Daddy didn't want to come home, it was that he couldn't come home. There were still bad men in Iraq; Daddy's job was to get rid of them, and his job wasn't over yet.

Marie seemed to accept the explanation, but later that morning, when Kristina corrected her daughter for a minor infraction, Marie flew into a rage. Kristina put her in her room and shut the door, waiting for her fury to subside. She heard Marie punching and kicking the walls, screaming, "I want my daddy!" Kristina started to go to her, but changed her mind, deciding that as long as Marie was screaming for her father, she would leave her to it. Kristina knew that she had needed time to scream for Scott, so she didn't see why her daughter shouldn't have the same opportunity. Marie sobbed for almost half an hour; Kristina went to her only when she heard her daughter's cries for "Daddy!" change to "Mama!"

The next week another one of Scott's boxes arrived, but this time it was no longer a hopeful reminder of his homecoming. Now, as Kristina sorted through the box and figured out what to keep and what to send back to Iraq, it was a cruel reminder of his continuing absence and the long months of loneliness and fear that remained.

CHAPTER FIFTEEN

"I want to start out by telling everyone how proud I am of both the soldiers and the family members of the 2ⁿᵈ Brigade Combat Team. These are extraordinary times in which we find ourselves and we are handling our current challenge extraordinarily well.

When the Department of the Army announced that 1ˢᵗ Armored Division would be extended, that news was a shock and a disappointment to everyone. It is a testament to the great soldiers and family members we have in 2BCT that everyone has received the news of our extension with such grace, poise, and professionalism."

—Col. Ralph A. Baker,
commander of Baumholder's 2ⁿᵈ Brigade Combat Team[1]

THANKS, SECRETARY RUMSFELD

In the days and weeks following the extension, spouses heard a lot from their husbands' commanders about sticking together as a community and the important role they played in support of the mission. The commanders admitted that the news had been a blow to soldiers and family members alike, but said that they also knew how strong the Baumholder community was and that working together, military families could get through anything. The troops needed their support; now was the time to pull together.

No one heard that message more clearly than Jena, who found out about the extension while she and some friends were at the battalion headquarters, filling up goodie bags for the soldiers. A soldier from the rear detachment approached the industrious group of women and informed them that an emergency meeting was going to be held that afternoon. Jena knew immediately. "So they won't be coming home," she said, setting down her bags.

She was crushed. Another four months in Iraq meant that Adam was going to miss his little sister's wedding, which had already been postponed twice in order for him to be able to attend. It could not be rescheduled a third time. Their vacation plans would have to be cancelled, and he was going to miss Jena's birthday for the third year in a row. Of course, none of that really mattered; what mattered was another four months of separation and danger.

Jena went home, sunk into a hot bath, and cried, but after only a few hours she forced herself to snap out of it. She took out the tape Adam had made for her before the deployment and slid it into the cassette player. Adam had told her just before he left to listen to the tape whenever she got lonely. In the first few months of his absence she had listened to it nightly, but lately she took it out less often. She played it only when she really needed it, and she certainly needed it now. She sat back on the couch, drying her eyes with a tissue, and listened as Adam's voice filled the living room, telling her how much he loved her, how much he appreciated her, and how proud he was of her. The words never failed to give her comfort. Inspired by his faith in her, Jena resolved to be the strong, courageous wife Adam needed her to be; wallowing in self-pity wasn't going to get him home any sooner. She reminded herself that she believed in her husband and she believed in his mission; the extension was simply an unfortunate but entirely understandable part of life in today's thinly stretched Army.

That evening Jena scheduled a meeting with some friends from the FRG so that they could start planning how best to use the next few months.

"There is a hidden blessing in this," she told her friends. "We were so rushed before. We kept saying that we needed more time to do things right for the homecoming. Now we can plan the best homecoming ever."

Jena knew that her positive spin on the extension was not shared by many of her peers, several of whom demanded information from rear detachment leaders. That, from Jena's perspective, showed how poorly they understood the nature of the work their husbands were doing in Iraq. They wanted to know when the soldiers were coming home, where they were moving to, and what, exactly, their new mission was going to be. Asking those questions was futile, Jena thought, not only because the information was classified but also because, in all likelihood, the commanders themselves didn't have the answers. To her way of thinking, none of this was hard to understand. Adam's work in Iraq wasn't over, and while she might not like the extension, there was no way she was not going to support it. She had to; that was just what Army wives did.

Tasha, whose reaction to the extension was more representative of a majority of spouses in Baumholder, could not have disagreed more. "I was living for April 1st," she said, explaining that for the past year she had kept that date in her mind as the day when she could start to breathe again. Now that day had come and gone, and she was just as scared and tired as she had ever been.

For Tasha, who described getting the news of the extension as "a punch in the chest," the rationale behind the extra months of perilous duty made little difference; extending 20,000 troops after they had already served one year in combat trampled on the sacrifice the soldiers and family members had already made. She could not believe they had gotten so near to closing this chapter of their lives only to have it drag on through yet another summer. "We were within seven days," she said, wiping away her tears. She and Keisha had made all the signs, covered bed sheets and poster boards with welcome home messages. Now, the signs were put away and she and Keisha were back to waiting.

"[The Bush administration doesn't] know how it feels to sit for twelve months and pray you're not the one who gets that notification and then be told that it's not enough," she said. "I'm human, I'm pissed off, and I just want my husband home. I'm so angry that it takes all of my being not to scream."

Tasha's anguish was reiterated in the *Stars and Stripes* newspaper, where every day another irate letter appeared in the opinion section as spouses railed against the extension. This letter to the editor, published on April 13th, 2004 was typical:

I'd like to extend a hearty thank you to Defense Secretary
Donald Rumsfeld for the pending 120-day extension of our
troops in Iraq. After all, what's another 120 days, really? For
our family it's four birthdays (again), Mother's Day and
Father's Day (again), our wedding anniversary (again), and
the Fourth of July, which is what service is all about for a lot
of military families.

I thank Secretary Rumsfeld for all of his talk about not
overburdening families and soldiers. One year of their lives on
the line, worrying daily about their safety, couldn't possibly be
enough to "overburden" us.

Thanks from our children, who apparently don't need a
father present, who cry when Mommy's time is not enough for
the four of them, who were counting the days until Daddy
could hold them on his lap.

Thanks for betraying our trust by telling us one year
"boots on the ground" and changing it at your discretion.
...Thanks for not sending help in the form of more troops last
spring when soldiers were dying, but keeping our soldiers
there for extra time this spring.

Thanks for the lies you spew about how things are not so
bad and we don't need more troops, all the while keeping 1ˢᵗ
Armored Division troops there....

The final thanks will be from whoever has to rebuild our
Army's strength when my husband and many others refuse to
reenlist.

I support our troops. I love my husband. We should not
have to choose the Army or family. We should be able to trust
that we can have [the] Army and family.
— Jessica Moretz, Geissen, Germany

In the weeks after the extension was announced—the same
weeks that were supposed to have been filled with joyful reunions
and family vacations—stunned spouses went about their days like
zombies, canceling vacation plans, taking down welcome home
banners, and throwing out spoiled food that no one had been
able to eat. Some of those with young children stared bitterly at

the paper link chains they had made at the start of the deployment to help their children understand how long it would be.
They had made 365 links, one for each day of the deployment
they had been told to expect, and instructed their kids to tear one
off every day. The chains that had once been piled high in the
corner had shriveled to almost nothing, so now what were they
going to do? Add on another 120 links and hope their children
wouldn't notice? It seemed that the mood on post could not get
any worse until, on April 29th, it did. Death returned to
Baumholder, and this time it came in droves.

A COMMUNITY IN MOURNING

At the time of the extension, soldiers from the Baumholder
community had suffered relatively few casualties. Since their arrival in the region in late April 2003, five soldiers had been killed
in combat, and seven others had died due to what the Department of Defense referred to as "nonhostile gunshot wounds" and
"noncombat-related injuries" such as accidental gunfire, vehicular
collisions, and suicides. Many others had been wounded, and while
the residents of Baumholder mourned each loss and injury, the
community as a whole felt grateful that so many of their loved
ones had survived the deployment physically unscathed.

News of an extension brought newfound worries, and family
members feared that increased combat missions in some of Iraq's
most dangerous cities could result in a rise in casualties. As
Baumholder's soldiers vacated the base that had been their home
for the past year and moved out to hotbeds of the insurgency,
communication was dramatically curtailed. Soldiers lost access
to email and phone calls were as rare as they had been the previous summer, when most soldiers had been able to contact their
families only once every couple weeks. With no direct source of
information, many spouses once again kept their television sets
tuned to CNN 24 hours a day. Images of the First Armored Division flooded their screens with the ghostly green of night vision
lenses. Jittery spouses strained to make out the faces of soldiers
as they appeared, fleetingly, on camera, wondering if the soldier

who had just run by with his rifle at chest level might be her husband and hoping that, whoever he was, he would make it safely through the night. No one could stand to think about the possibility of a casualty now, at a time when the soldiers should already have been home.

On April 29th, soldiers from C Battery, 4th Battalion, 27th Field Artillery Regiment were on security duty along a road south of Baghdad when a suicide bomber detonated a station wagon filled with explosives. Several soldiers were wounded, two of them seriously. Eight soldiers were killed in the attack.[2]

It was the worst possible scenario, Lt. Col. Michael Cerrone, a Baumholder chaplain, said in an article in the *Stars and Stripes*.[3] With the recent extension and the deaths of two soldiers earlier in April, the past month had already been exceedingly difficult for the Baumholder community. Now, with eight soldiers from one platoon killed in a single incident, everyone's worst fears had been realized.

The day of the memorial service was appropriately gray and gloomy, threatening rain as family members and soldiers filed into the standing room only chapel. This was not the first memorial service for a fallen soldier in Baumholder, but for many, it was the hardest to witness. Eight empty helmets and eight sets of empty combat boots lined the front of the chapel, never to be worn again, and eight times a soldier called out for men who would never answer. In a single day, more soldiers from Baumholder had been killed than all previous combat deaths combined, and the community mourned the loss of so many of its own.

Commanders asked community members not to cheapen the deaths of its fallen soldiers with talk that they should have been home by now; to do so, they said, was disrespectful of both the mission and the soldiers' sacrifice. Heeding their instructions, few voiced their opinions in public, but privately, a single thought ran through everyone's mind: If it weren't for the extension, all eight of those soldiers would still be alive.

The next morning, Beth was in the bathroom when she heard the doorbell ring.

"I'll be right there!" she called out, but Kathryn ran ahead of her, inching the door open just a crack. Beth hurried to the door and pulled Kathryn out of the way—clearly they needed to have another talk about not opening the door for strangers—and caught a glimpse of a male shoulder draped in dark green. Her pulse surged and her grip tightened around Kathryn's arm. This couldn't be happening. Doug couldn't be dead; she refused to believe it. But why else would the soldier be standing on her doorstep?

With unsteady hands she opened the door the rest of the way, revealing a smiling soldier dressed not in a Class A uniform, as she had feared, but standard green camouflage BDUs. "Hi!" he said cheerfully. "I'm your new neighbor. I just moved in a few days ago and I noticed the announcement that you have a car for sale. I was wondering if I could take a look at it."

Beth laughed nervously as she tried to regain her composure. "The car. Of course! Come on in." It took more than an hour for her hands to stop shaking.

GOD GIVES WHAT YOU ASK FOR, NOT WHAT YOU WANT

When Diane learned the identity of the eight fallen soldiers, she immediately called her mother to tell her that Thomas was not among the dead. She assumed that so many soldiers being killed in a single day would have made the headlines back home and didn't want her mother to worry. But when Diane told her the news her mother informed her that all she had seen about the deadly attack was a line in the news ticker at the bottom of her television screen as a reporter gave exhaustive details of the latest developments in the Michael Jackson child abuse allegations. It was hard for Diane to imagine a world in which soldier's deaths were not front-page news. In Baumholder, she said, "We live, eat, and breathe Iraq." There was no escaping it.

Diane had been on edge ever since she got the news about the extension, and now, with the deaths of those eight soldiers, she was overwhelmed with self-reproach and guilt. She chastised herself for wishing that Thomas would not come home, half believing that her fantasy had somehow led to the extension. She now realized that she had never really wanted him to stay away, she had just wanted to avoid the "tough stuff" that they were going to have to deal with once he came home. But, she thought regretfully, God gives you what you ask for, not what you want. Now she wanted him to come home more than anything; nothing they would face upon his return could be worse than the possibility of his never coming home at all.

The sudden lack of communication made the weeks seem interminable. She and Thomas had come to depend on nightly email exchanges, but those days were over; all they had now were brief, occasional phone calls filled with well-intended lies. Diane knew that her petty concerns were nothing compared to what Thomas was facing. When she was tired or bored she could rent a movie, go get a pizza, and take a warm bath to unwind. Thomas could do none of those things, nor could he ever, for one moment, forget about where he was or the danger he was in. So when he called she would lie and say that everything was fine at home, which wasn't really so much of a lie after all, compared to what they had been through a few months ago. And he lied back, assuring her that he was safe and doing well. So we're just going to lie to each other for the next few months, she thought. Then we'll let it all come out when he comes home. *If* he comes home.

CHAPTER SIXTEEN

"Those who have long enjoyed such privileges as we enjoy forget in time that men have died to win them."
—*Franklin D. Roosevelt*

"Men will not fight and die without knowing what they are fighting and dying for."
—*General Douglas MacArthur*

THE NOTIFICATION

Now that the division had been gone over a year, commanders were telling soldiers to call home to get their affairs in order; powers of attorney, good for up to one year, had to be extended, and if anyone needed to update a will, now was the time to do it. Jena's husband made his call in early May, and after a quick "I love you" and "Don't worry about me" Adam took out his list. The list was mostly mundane household items affected by the extension. Jena took notes as he dictated, but when he got to his will she balked. "You can't ask me about that!" she screamed in a rare, uncontrolled moment of panic. His staying in Iraq for another three or four months was one thing; thinking about the possibility of his never coming home was another.

Two days later, Jena was strolling home from walking the dog when she noticed an official U.S. Army car carrying two soldiers in Class A uniforms heading toward her street. She felt her pulse quicken and, without meaning to, she started doing the math: If the soldiers stopped at her building there was a one-in-twenty-four chance that Adam was dead; if they stopped at her stairwell, it was one-in-eight. Don't come down here, she prayed silently. Please let it be somebody else. The car turned before it reached her street and she exhaled, surprised to find that she had been holding her breath.

Baumholder was still reeling from the April 29th carnage when news of another casualty swept post. On May 3rd an insurgent shot and killed Staff Sergeant Eric Petty. He was 28 years old, and he left behind a wife and son. Less than three weeks later the community was in mourning again. On May 21st Jeremy Horton, a 24-year-old staff sergeant, was killed when his vehicle ran over a roadside bomb. It was Staff Sergeant Horton's wife, Christie, who opened her front door to find the soldiers in Class A's Jena had seen on her walk.

For Teresa, news of Staff Sergeant Horton's death hit especially close to home. Christie Horton had been a member of her FRG, and even though Staff Sergeant Horton had since been transferred to a different unit, Christie had retained close ties with the wives in his old battalion. For the first time, the widow was not a faceless stranger but someone Teresa actually knew, and that made the news of his death more real to her than any other.

Teresa, Heather, and Jennifer attended the memorial service together and afterward went to Shooters, a local burger joint, hoping that the empty calories and grease might absorb some of their sadness. "God bless her," Jennifer repeated like a mantra. Teresa was silent for a long time, searching for words to express a complicated tangle of emotions: sorrow, pity, anger, relief, guilt. Then, shaking salt onto a mound of french fries, she confessed that as sorry as she felt about Christie's loss, all throughout the service she had been thanking God that she was not the one sitting up there in the front pew. Heather and Jennifer nodded their heads slowly. "Hopefully we'll never be there," they said, immediately assuring one another that they never would be. There had been too much death already; surely Staff Sergeant Horton would be the last soldier from Baumholder to die.

They were wrong. By the end of the month, Teresa, Heather, and Jennifer would attend another memorial service, and this time, they would be the ones seated in the front of the chapel.

On the last Saturday in May, the three friends were in the midst of another busy weekend—their weekly get-together on Friday night, a Riesling wine tasting on Saturday, and a free Toby Keith and Ted Nugent concert for troops and their families on Sunday. It was all part of the plan; now that romantic getaways with husbands had been cancelled, staying busy was more important than ever. Teresa, Heather, and Jennifer packed their schedules with as many pick-me-ups as possible, filling their evenings and weekends with movie dates, girls' nights out, and shopping trips in search of "va va va voom" outfits to surprise their husbands with once they finally returned from Iraq.

Jennifer backed out of the wine tasting at the last minute in order to nurse a burgeoning migraine, so Teresa and Heather went off without her, returning several hours later to check on how she was feeling. Jennifer was beaming when she opened the door. Not only had her migraine subsided, her husband, Rob, had called. It had been a while since they had last talked and their 10th anniversary was right around the corner, so she was especially glad that she had been home to receive his call. Rob told her that in case he wasn't able to call again between now and then, he wanted to wish her a happy anniversary in advance, and promised to call again just as soon as he could.

The friends said goodnight, agreeing to meet the following evening to get ready for the concert. Teresa woke early the next morning to hit the books. She had fallen hopelessly behind on her course work while Danny was home and needed every minute before the concert to catch up. Several hours later her studies were interrupted by a phone call. Jennifer's voice came into the receiver, shaky and tearful. "Rob was injured," she gasped into the phone.

"I'll be right over," Teresa said, reaching for her keys.

By the time she got to Jennifer's apartment, several other friends were already gathered in the living room, trying to piece together the few sketchy details they had. There had been a mortar attack on the compound, and Rob had gone out with a group of scouts to respond to the attack. Somewhere en route, the vehicle Rob was riding in had hit an IED. He and another soldier, Sergeant Aaron Elandt, had been badly injured. It looked as though

Rob was going to survive the attack, but his injuries were severe; even if he lived, he would never be the same again.

Teresa, Heather, and Jennifer talked late into the night, discussing possible scenarios, trying to plan for the unimaginable. Rob's injuries would probably mean the end of his promising career in the Army, but there were plenty of other things that he could do, and Jennifer would be there to help him. The important thing was that Rob was still alive; Jennifer was strong and together they could deal with whatever came next once he was home.

Finally, just past dawn, they got an update. The doctors were taking Rob off the respirator. That had to be a good sign, the friends agreed. But as five tedious, nerve-racking hours passed without new information, their hope began to dim.

That afternoon the doorbell rang. Expecting someone from the FRG, Teresa and another friend from the battalion, a company commander's wife named Carrie[1], jumped up to answer the door. When they opened it Teresa was surprised to find Captain Jim Hoffman, the rear detachment commander for their battalion, accompanied by an Army chaplain.

"Hi!" Teresa said cheerfully when she saw Jim. "What are you doing here?"

Carrie stared at the men for a long moment, taking in their starched, dark green uniforms and the rainbows of colored ribbons pinned neatly across their chests. Wordlessly, she slammed the door in their faces. "Shit!" she said, the color draining from her cheeks.

"What are you doing?" Teresa asked uncomprehendingly. "That's Jim."

Carrie opened the door again, just a crack, but again slammed it shut. "Shit!" she said again. "Shit! Shit! Shit!" Finally, she opened the door a third time and allowed the two grave-faced men in Class A uniforms to enter.

Just as the men entered the living room, Heather glanced up from the card game she and Jennifer had been playing to pass the time. She knew at once what their arrival meant and collapsed onto the floor in shock, sobbing uncontrollably. Friends grabbed her and pulled her into the bedroom as Jim and the chaplain approached Jennifer, whose face registered first shock, then horror as the soldiers sat down gingerly on the couch opposite her to deliver their awful message.

Meanwhile Teresa, still refusing to accept what Jennifer already understood, followed Heather into the bedroom. "No, no, it's okay," she said soothingly. "It's probably just a coma, that all. That's why Jim's here. They probably just wanted to have a chaplain here in case she falls apart. Rob is going to be fine. Really. He'll be fine."

Another friend took Teresa gently by the arm and said, "No Teresa. That's not why he's here."

"No, no," Teresa insisted, moving toward Heather, but as soon as she reached her distraught friend reality finally set in.

Rob was dead, and Jennifer was a widow. That was why Jim was here. Teresa fell into Heather's arms and cried.

Two days later Teresa stood in the center of the chapel, supervising the memorial service rehearsal so that Jennifer would not have to endure the ceremony twice. The service was to be held in honor of both Rob and the 23-year-old scout, Aaron Elandt, who had also succumbed to his injuries from the attack. As Teresa went through the motions of the rehearsal, confirming who would speak for which soldier and when, she was startled to realize that she had not thought about Danny once in the past few days. She had been so consumed with anguish for Jennifer that Danny had slipped out of the picture completely. Her head swam with punishing, guilt-ridden thoughts. Why did she deserve to have a husband while Jennifer's was dead? How could she have allowed herself to take Danny's presence in her life for granted?

At 11 a.m. on Friday, June 4th, Teresa, Heather, and Jennifer assembled at the side entrance of the chapel, once again dressed in the dark colors of mourning, once again bracing themselves for roll call and "Taps" and the rifle volley salute, but this time, they would be the ones heading to the front of the chapel. Teresa walked briskly down the center aisle, passing Jena and Tasha, who were seated separately in the back of the chapel. She kept her eyes trained on the carpet, acknowledging no one as she took her seat. Jennifer followed, moving slowly, almost serenely, toward her designated place in the front pew. The same women who had once gathered around Teresa's Thanksgiving table and prayed for their husbands' safe return surrounded her on either side, scooting close as if to buffer their grief-stricken friend against the agonizing ritual. Their best intentions were trumped by sorrow, and by the time the first sergeant stood up to read roll call, everyone was in tears.

"Captain Scheetz!" the first sergeant called.
Silence.

"Captain Robert Scheetz!" he called again.
Silence.

"Captain Robert Charles Scheetz!"

When the bugler sounded the first notes of "Taps" it was almost a relief; anything to end the heartbreaking silence of a soldier, son, friend, and husband who would never again raise his voice to respond to the call.

SUMMER, AGAIN

"Recruiting for the United States Army is going to be a major challenge in the days ahead," Representative Ike Skelton of Missouri, the senior Democrat on the House Armed Services Committee, said this week. "You are wearing them out."

—New York Times[1]

CHAPTER SEVENTEEN

"When troops are deployed, when they are being wounded, when they are being killed, it's tough.... The families that are left behind are an important part of the network that supports one another. What impressed me was their resolve. They understand, like the military members, how important this deployment is."
—*Joint Chiefs Chairman Air Force Gen. Richard B. Myers,
speaking at a press conference following a visit
with Baumholder families, June 6, 2004*

"BODIES"

Two days after the memorial service, General Richard B. Myers, chairman of the Joint Chiefs of Staff, came to Baumholder to deliver a message of encouragement and thanks. The extra months soldiers were spending in Iraq were a sacrifice that he understood and appreciated, and their work had not been in vain. First Armored Division soldiers had made significant gains in places like Najaf and Karbala in recent weeks. "Thank God for the First Armored Division," he said.

The audience, which had been restricted to soldiers in the rear detachment, FRG leaders, and one additional senior spouse per company, hung on his every word, waiting for some assurance that the soldiers really were coming home this time. The anticipated length of the extension had recently been reduced from 120 days to 90 and the end was once again in sight, but no one on post was prepared to get her hopes up. The Department of Defense had extended the troops once before. There was no reason to think they wouldn't do it again, and many spouses feared that if the soldiers didn't get out of Iraq before the potentially explosive change of sovereignty on June 30th, they might get stuck there even longer.

General Myers opened up the meeting to questions, and hands shot up across the room.

"Can you give us a date for when First Armored Division soldiers will be coming home?" one woman asked.

"I can't give you an exact date," the general replied. "But I can tell you that we will get your husbands home as soon as the mission permits."

"Is there any chance that, once the 90 day extension is up, the soldiers could be extended again?" another spouse wanted to know.

"A second extension is extremely unlikely, although forces on the ground can always change that forecast," the general hedged. "That was what happened back in April. The decision to extend troops beyond their one-year tour was one that no one wanted to make, but the Army simply needed more bodies."

"Bodies?" one woman whispered heatedly to a friend seated next to her. Everyone at the meeting had been part of the Army community long enough to know what the general meant by "bodies." In the Army vernacular, "bodies" was simply another way of referring to soldiers, similar to the way "boots on the ground" was used to refer to a mass military presence. But two soldiers from Baumholder had been killed in the past week; they hadn't even been buried yet. Following so closely on the heels of the post's bloodiest months of battle, the casual reference struck many in the room as an ominous indication of just how expendable their husbands' lives had become.

Meanwhile, at a Hooligan's restaurant in the Atlanta airport, Teresa, Heather, and Jennifer sat in a booth, waiting to begin the last leg of a sorrowful journey. They were on their way to a funeral. Teresa and Heather were accompanying Jennifer back to the United States to bury Rob.

"Let's get margaritas," Jennifer suggested. Teresa and Heather looked up in surprise; margaritas didn't seem to fit the somber mood. Neither knew what to expect from Jennifer on this trip, whether she would try to make the best of things despite the heartbreaking circumstances or if she would collapse with grief. Her suggestion seemed to indicate the former. "Margaritas were Rob's favorite drink," Jennifer explained. "I just think that we should have one in his honor."

An overly cheerful, middle-aged waiter sidled up to their table. "So, you ladies on a vacation?" he asked.

"No," Teresa snapped, hoping he would get the hint, take their drink order, and leave.

The waiter persisted. "Visiting family?"

"You could say that," Teresa answered abruptly.

"So where you headin'?" he asked, oblivious to her monotone replies. "Gonna do any travelin' while ya'll are here? Where ya'll from, anyway?"

Jennifer shot Teresa and Heather an exasperated look. "Germany," she answered.

"Germany? That's great!" the waiter exclaimed. "What do ya'll do over there?"

"Look," Teresa said at last. "Could we order some drinks?"

When the margaritas came at last, Jennifer raised her glass in a toast. "To Rob," she said in a faltering voice.

"To Rob," Teresa and Heather echoed, fighting back their own tears. They didn't feel right about crying in front of Jennifer. It was her tragedy, not theirs, and they were supposed to be there to help her. But they often found themselves overcome by emotion.

Teresa tried to keep things light over the meal. She desperately wanted to see Jennifer smile again, and saw it as her role to keep her friend from dwelling too much on her mourning. But how, she wondered, do you make the best of a funeral?

Their flight was announced and Teresa excused herself to find the waiter. "I'm sorry if we were rude back there," she told him as she handed him her credit card. "We're on our way to a funeral. That woman over there, my friend, her husband was just killed in Iraq, so we're not really in a festive mood."

"Oh," the waiter said, suddenly at a loss for words. "Oh, God. I'm really sorry."

"Yeah...well," Teresa stammered. She didn't know what to say either.

Teresa and Heather never left Jennifer's side during the emotionally exhausting trip, and by the time they returned to Baumholder Jennifer had decided to stay in the apartment she and Rob had shared until the soldiers who had served with him returned home. Her time back in the States had proven to her that it was here, in the Army community, where she needed to be. This was where her best friends were—friendships that had grown even deeper through tragedy—and she needed their support more than ever. Furthermore, over a year had passed since she had last seen Rob, and even after the memorial service and funeral it was still hard to accept that his continuing absence wasn't simply a result of the extension. Seeing Rob's fellow soldiers return without him was the only way to make his death seem real. Leaving Baumholder before the deployment was over felt strangely like quitting; for Rob's sake as much as her own, she had to see it through to the end.

Jennifer's father came out to help her get her affairs in order: filling out masses of paperwork, scheduling the shipment of her household goods, the agonizing task of sorting through Rob's uniforms and medals and deciding what to keep and what to give away. Teresa and Heather tried to maintain some semblance of normalcy. They continued their evening walks, went to the movies, and took her out to dinner several times a week. But of course, none of it felt the same.

Now that the extension had dropped from 120 days to 90 days, most soldiers from Baumholder were expected to arrive in mid to late July, only a few weeks away. All around them people were starting to get excited again, an excitement that, for the three friends, brought only added sorrow. As much as Teresa looked forward to seeing Danny again, at getting a second chance to do their reunion right, she was consumed by Jennifer's loss. For most Baumholder residents the deployment was almost over, and that was wonderful, but what about all the families of soldiers who weren't ever coming home?

A TIME OF RENEWAL

Jena, too, was doing a lot of thinking about the soldiers who weren't coming home. The memorial service for Captain Scheetz and Staff Sergeant Elandt had shaken her. It was only a matter of chance that Adam had not been a part of that convoy; she could easily have been the one to get the awful news. She didn't know Jennifer very well, but she had often observed her at FRG meetings and admired the poise with which she conducted herself. Jena had always thought of Jennifer as the very model of an army wife: positive, always willing to help, unfailingly stoic, and loyal to both her husband and the Army.

Jena often reflected on a conversation she'd had with Jennifer as they picked up boxes from their husbands in the community mailroom. Only days before Jennifer's husband was killed she had talked about how excited she was to see him again and all the plans she had for block leave. It seemed unbelievably cruel that all that hope and excitement could have been snatched away so quickly.

Jennifer had seemed so calm at the memorial service, Jena thought, almost as if she were the one comforting those around her instead of the other way around. Jena prayed she would never find herself in that position, and if she did, she hoped she could hold up half as well. But watching Jennifer take that long, lonely walk down the chapel's center aisle had upset some of Jena's most basic assumptions. "I have always had this pie in the sky ideal that what we were doing in Iraq was worth the ultimate sacrifice," Jena said after the memorial service, but suddenly that ideal had been called into question. If Adam were killed in action, could she really say that his death was worthwhile? She hoped so, but looking at those two helmets and two empty pairs of combat boots at the front of the chapel and so many tear-stained faces had left her feeling uncertain about how she would react if it were Adam's helmet and boots up there instead of someone else's.

For the time being, Jena tried to put those unsettling questions out of her mind. Assuming nothing horrible happened to prevent it, Adam was coming home in a few weeks, and she wanted to do everything she could to be ready. On a rainy June morning, she followed a trickle of spouses into the FRG community meeting room, a cavernous, unadorned space resembling a high school cafeteria. A few young wives had gathered around the buffet table, filling plates of food for themselves and their children as they waited for the "Romance and Reunion" training to begin. The training was part of an ongoing series sponsored by Army Community Services, which had flown in a team of social workers and family counselors to help Baumholder spouses prepare, yet again, for the imminent return of the soldiers. The first flights out of the Middle East were scheduled to leave within weeks, and once again Baumholder was a flurry of activity in preparation for the soldiers' arrival.

Jena got to the meeting room just past the scheduled 8:30 a.m. start time, took a piece of toast and jam from the buffet, carefully avoiding the tempting sausage and bacon, and sat down at one of the nearly empty tables. Even though she did not anticipate any major problems when Adam came home, she had been through so much lately—her grandmother's illness, the extension, the recent deaths of two soldiers from Adam's unit—that she thought it would be a good idea to learn what she could from the experts.

One of the counselors, a slim, energetic male social worker, eased into the session with a role-play, then got to his main point. "Resentment equals poison," he said firmly, and the small group of women gathered around the table nodded their heads intently. "Rebuilding intimacy after more than a year apart is a challenge," he continued, "and the only way to do it is to let go of resentment, both real and imagined, preferably *before* your husbands come home."

He went on to warn the women to be careful about their expectations. "Fantasies are great," he cautioned, "but they can get you into trouble, especially when it comes to sex. Their needs and your needs are going to be a little bit off."

A young woman with two small children, one sleeping soundly on her lap, sighed knowingly. "Yeah," she said. "*Way* off."

It's true, Jena thought as she reflected back on Adam's return from basic training. They had already been married two years at the time, and in terms of sex there wasn't much that was new between them anymore, but after months of separation she had felt an almost virginal shyness around Adam. It had taken time for them to relearn the intimacy that only a few months before had seemed so natural.

Jena jotted down notes as the social workers doled out advice about improving communication, guarding against typical reunion pitfalls of unrealistic expectations and crowding, and recognizing signs of emotional trauma. "The real danger for marriages," the social worker warned, "comes not from the trauma of war but from the emotional separation it creates. In order to survive the past year, couples have needed to distance themselves emotionally. Now you are going to have to rebuild that emotional intimacy, and it won't be easy." Reunions, he said, while wonderful and joyful in many ways, could also be a time of severe stress for couples and families.

"I'm sure there will be a lot of marriages that don't survive this," another counselor predicted somberly. Some of the women at the table glanced at one another nervously and, noting their discomfort, she quickly continued, "But remember, this can also be a time for renewal. You had no control over what happened in Iraq, but you do have control over what you do as a couple."

SOMETHING NEEDS TO CHANGE

Kristina longed for the day when she would have control over her life again. Even with Scott's scheduled return date weeks away, she couldn't allow herself to believe that the whole ordeal might soon be over. Memories of his last anticipated homecoming and the crushing disappointment that followed were still too fresh for that. She vowed not to hang a single welcome home banner until she knew his plane was on the ground, and she did the best she could to put the homecoming out of her mind entirely. It was self-preservation mode, she explained to friends; she wasn't about to let herself get burned twice.

She and Scott had fallen out of contact once again, this time through no fault of his own. Once his company left its established base Scott lost regular phone and email access. Most of their computer equipment had been packed up and shipped off in preparation for redeployment and once they found out about the extension, it had been too late to get it back. Even if they had the equipment, it would have done him little good. The division was on the move, going wherever the insurgency demanded; all of the comforts they had come to enjoy in the past year were gone.

Kristina felt the effects of the decreased communication in her marriage. Scott had been gone so long that she often said that she couldn't even remember what it felt like to be a family anymore, and she knew that, despite the progress they had made during R&R, they were going to have a lot to work on when he came home. So much had been repressed, overlooked, and even forgotten during his long absence, and it was going to take a lot of work to get past that. Marie was going to preschool now, Tyler was walking and had even started to talk, and Scott had missed all of it except for 15 days back in January. It was no way to live. Worse yet, people in Baumholder were already talking about the next deployment to Iraq. Soldiers would be home for a year, maybe less, and could be back in Iraq as early as summer 2005.

"Something needs to change," she told Scott during one of his rare phone calls that summer.

"I know," Scott agreed. "You're right. As soon as my enlistment contract is up, I'm done. I'm getting out of the Army."

Kristina spent the last weeks of June researching alternative careers: state trooper, private security guard, or even something with one of the paramilitary companies. She wished Scott had other, safer, options. Unfortunately, his military experience didn't qualify him for much that transferred to the civilian world. But as dangerous as the alternatives were, at least he wouldn't have to miss more than a year of their lives again. At least he would be around to see his children grow up and he would generally be home for at least one meal a day. To Kristina, just about anything sounded like a huge improvement over the life in the Army; their family simply couldn't take another year like this one.

CHAPTER EIGHTEEN

"Are we excited? I can't hear you! Are we excited?"
—*A representative from Army Community Services*
pumps up the crowd at one of the first
welcome home ceremonies in Baumholder, July 8, 2004

BLESSED IN NEW WAYS

On a warm summer morning Tasha and Keisha walked into the church on Ramstein Air Base for the teen choir's anniversary celebration. It was the last time the group would all be together. Due to summer vacation the choir would not meet regularly for the next few months, and by the time it reconvened, Tasha and Keisha would be gone. Anthony would be home soon, and as soon as he came back the family was moving to Fort Hood, Texas, where he and Tasha planned to start building a house and eventually retire.

The teens, all wearing matching t-shirts emblazoned with the words *Blessed in New Ways*, the choir motto, pulled Tasha up to the podium to express their gratitude for the work she had done. One by one they presented her with a single rose to place in an elaborate cut glass vase they had all chipped in to buy.

"We went through a lot of misery together, Ms. Washington" one of the girls on Tasha's call list whispered as she handed her a rose, "but we made it." Tasha squeezed the girl's hand and blinked back a tear. The girl spoke the truth. During the past year they had all been through their share of trials, and the weekly practices had been as important to Tasha as they had to any of the teens. These kids had become like her own, taking her mind off her own problems and giving her strength to carry on, even on her hardest days.

After the ceremony, the church pastor asked the teens to come forward with their parents. It was part of a ceremony the church held annually to bring teens and parents together, in front of God and the congregation, to recommit to building a positive relationship. As the parents and children approached the podium, many holding hands and wiping away tears, Tasha turned to Keisha, wondering if they should go up there as they had the previous year. They had not always had an easy relationship. Tasha was a strict disciplinarian and demanded high standards from her only daughter. She knew that it couldn't always be easy for the girl. The past few years had been especially difficult, as she and Keisha had tried to find their places in a family bigger than just the two of them.

"We don't have to do that," Keisha said in answer to her mother's unspoken question. "We're okay this time." Tasha took her hand and smiled. Keisha was right, Tasha thought. We are okay. At least there was one good thing to come out of this miserable experience.

That evening, Keisha confided in Tasha that, for the first time, she wasn't worried about what their relationship would be like when Anthony came home. After more than a year alone with her mother, she felt ready to accept Anthony as a full member of their family; in fact, she was looking forward to having him back. Their family was going to make it; she felt sure of that now.

Tasha looked at her daughter quizzically. She knew Keisha had grown up a lot in the past year, and that having the time alone together had strengthened the mother-daughter bond that had been weakened by her marriage, but this was quite a proclamation for a teenage girl to make.

"Grandma Effie told me," Keisha explained. "She visited me in a dream a few weeks ago." The grandmother Keisha referred to was actually Tasha's guardian, a matriarch from a small North Carolina farming community who had raised Tasha from early childhood into adulthood. She had also had a hand in raising Keisha. When Tasha was on orders to deploy to the first Gulf War,

she had sent Keisha to live with her guardian until the deployment was over. She had been Tasha's dearest and most trusted
ally until her death several years earlier, and Tasha deeply missed
her advice and companionship. It was Tasha's guardian who had
assured her that she would be able to handle the challenges of
single parenthood when she discovered her unplanned and ill-
timed pregnancy, and it was also her guardian who had told her,
in a dream, that Anthony was the man she should spend the rest
of her life with. Tasha believed in the power of those nocturnal
visits, and during the long deployment she had often prayed that
her guardian would come to her in her sleep, but she never did.

"She visited you?" Tasha asked incredulously. "What did she
say?"

"She told me to be good and to be aware of what was goin' on
around me," Keisha said. "She told me that it was okay to love
Anthony and make our family work."

"But why didn't she come to me?" Tasha asked.

"She said you didn't need her like I did, " Keisha answered.
"She told me you were going to be okay."

HOMECOMING

By early July, the Baumholder community was once again
preparing to welcome its soldiers home. Several advance parties
had already returned to ecstatic welcomes, and the rest of
Baumholder's companies were expected back between mid-July
and early August. Once again, yellow ribbons adorned every tree
and signpost and posters blanketed buildings like graffiti. Several
industrious wives even lined the roads leading into post with signs
that read, "Getting warmer," and "You're almost home!"

As the countdown finally went from weeks to days Beth put
up a few welcome home signs and made sure the apartment was
in order but, hoping to avoid the deluge of anxious phone calls
asking "Is he home yet?" she remained intentionally vague with
friends and family members back home about Doug's return date.
She wanted to avoid getting her heart set on a day that might
come and go without her husband's arrival. As long as he was

home by August 15th, the last day of the original 120-day extension, she would be happy. At least, that was what she told herself
whenever excitement got the better of her. There was no sense in
getting her hopes up for anything sooner than that.

The soundness of her reasoning was soon borne out. On the
day Doug's flight was scheduled to arrive, the battalion
commander's wife, a woman Beth knew well from her work on
several FRG projects, called to inform her that there had been a
mechanical malfunction with the plane. All flights were on hold
for the time being.

"Are you okay?" she asked Beth.

"Yes, I'm okay," Beth answered honestly. She had never expected the flight to come in on schedule anyway.

Finally, after a series of false alarms, the much anticipated day
arrived. "They're coming!" Beth announced ecstatically to the
women on her telephone roster. "Meet at the Hall of Champions
at 12:30 p.m. for the ceremony." The FRG phone tree sprung into
action, and by morning, every wife in the battalion knew that a
planeload of soldiers was on its way home.

Beth took her time getting dressed that morning, choosing a
knee-length khaki skirt and a sleeveless maroon top that showed
off her slender figure, and then took out the special dress she had
chosen for Kathryn so many months ago.

"Where are we going Mommy?" Kathryn asked as Beth slipped
the dress over her head.

"We're going to an FRG meeting at the gym," Beth fibbed.
Kathryn would go berserk if she knew her father was coming
home and she thought it best to keep her daughter in the dark
until the last possible moment.

When they arrived at the Hall of Champions the gym was
teaming with expectant wives and children holding balloons, video
cameras, and welcome home signs. The walls were covered with
colorful poster board filled with messages reading, "Welcome
Home!", "Finally!", and "You're My Hero!" Large speakers set up
on either side of the bleachers blared Top 40 music, pumping up
the highly charged atmosphere even further.

Half an hour crawled past, but as the 12:30 arrival time drew nearer, cell phones started to ring. Beth knew the purpose of the calls without having to ask; there had been another delay. She glanced over at Kathryn, who was happily engaged in a game of tag with a group of children. Thank goodness she doesn't know what's going on, Beth thought; I'd have a monster on my hands.

Periodically a short, balding man from Army Community Services stepped up to the microphone and shouted, "Are we excited? I can't hear you! Are we excited?"

The crowd of women and children gave a half-hearted response, too wound up and anxious to be whipped into frenzy by this unlikely cheerleader.

"Don't tell me to be excited," one balloon-toting woman muttered. "Of course I'm excited. It's been over 14 months!"

Two hours past the scheduled arrival time, the balding man took the microphone again. He paused dramatically to make sure he had everyone's attention, then yelled, "They're here!" The first soldier appeared, walking briskly to the center of the gym floor as Toby Keith's patriotic hit song "Courtesy of the Red, White, and Blue (The Angry American)" filled the room and the crowd broke into ear-splitting hoots and whistles. One by one the soldiers marched into the gymnasium, stifling grins as they stole surreptitious glances into the crowd. By the time the last soldier had taken his place in the formation the gym was a cacophony of joyful shouting and applause, eager wives and children straining to distinguish their husband or father from the others. The soldiers continued to march in place until the first sergeant gave the order to stand at parade rest, and all 120 soldiers placed their arms behind their backs and faced the battalion commander as he took the microphone to congratulate them on a job well done.

"Kathryn," Beth whispered. "Daddy's here." Kathryn examined her mother's face incredulously.

"Which one's my daddy?" she asked, squirming out of Beth's arms to get a better look. "I don't see him. Where is he?"

"He's there," Beth said, pointing into the sea of nearly identical soldiers. "There, the second one from the end."

Kathryn pulled her small body as straight as she could to see over the crowd, but still couldn't tell him apart from the other soldiers gathered on the floor in front of her. "I don't see him!" she whined.

The battalion commander finished speaking, and the soldiers raised their right arms in salute as first the national anthem and then the Army song boomed from the loud speakers. Finally, after what seemed like an interminable wait, the song came to an end, and the first sergeant barked, "Dismissed!" The rope barrier that had separated the soldiers from their family members was pulled away and bright colors seeped into the tan mass of soldiers as both sides rushed forward, pushing through the crowd to meet in tearful embraces. Beth pushed her way through the euphoric crowd, searching for Doug. They met in a warm but short-lived family hug, for as soon as she could, Kathryn wriggled out of Beth's grasp and launched herself into her father's arms, clinging to him fiercely. She arched back to examine his face, making sure it was really him, and then giggled gleefully as she pressed her small body against his shoulder, her face an expression of pure bliss.

Turning to Beth she said, "I can't love you right now, Mommy."

"Why not, Kathryn?" Beth asked.

"I'm so full of love for my daddy that I don't love you right now," she said innocently, "but you can love me, Mommy, 'cause in a while I will feel better and I can love you again."

Beth fought back a laugh and, gazing lovingly at her daughter, cuddled against Doug's other shoulder, and wiped tears of joy and relief from her eyes. She could hardly believe it was real; after 14 months and 6 days, Doug was finally home.

Jena and Tasha were the next to get the call telling them that their husbands' plane had landed and that the time had come to go to the gym to welcome them home. Jena arrived at the Hall of Champions loaded down with magazines and puzzle books to keep her occupied during what she expected to be a lengthy wait. She found a seat in the bleachers and began flipping through one of the magazines she had brought, but the images in front of her barely registered; all she could think about was the fact that Adam would soon be walking through that door. Elsewhere in the crowd, Tasha nearly bounced with nervous energy as she tried to hold a conversation with her church pastor and his wife, who had come with her and Keisha to welcome home the longest-absent member of their congregation.

"Are you excited?" a woman from Army Community Services hollered into the microphone for the fourth time since they had arrived.

"She better not take that microphone again unless my husband is right outside that door," Tasha grumbled. But this time, there was a reason to get excited; less than a minute later the door flung open and soldiers streamed into the gym.

Again, the battalion commander stepped up to the microphone to praise the soldiers for their courage and tenacity, and again, eager family members entertained fantasies of breaking through the rope barrier separating them from their loved ones as they waited impatiently for the first sergeant's dismissal.

When the release order finally came, Tasha and Jena hurtled through the crowd to find their husbands. Tasha found Anthony first and clutched him tightly.

"I told you I'd be okay," Anthony chided as he returned her embrace. Only now that Tasha had her arms around him was she willing to believe it. Keisha grinned at them, wiping tears away from her eyes, then picked up her overnight bag and started to leave.

"You can stay, you know," Tasha told her. "You don't have to leave."

"I know," Keisha said. "I already checked him out. He's still got 10 fingers and 10 toes. I know he's fine. I'll see you in a couple of days." And with that she gave them another wave and headed off.

Nearby, Jena and Adam stood in the center of all the mayhem, oblivious to the crowd around them. "I love you so much," Jena whispered into the base of his neck. Adam pulled back and smiled, kissing away a tear making its way down Jena's cheek. Just then the throng of soldiers filtering out of the gymnasium caught Jena's attention and she suddenly remembered the bags of food she had waiting in the barracks. She had spent days cooking so that every single soldier on the flight would have a home-cooked meal to come home to, and she couldn't focus all of her attention on Adam until she knew the meals had been delivered. Jena and Adam clasped hands and set off for the barracks.

Soon afterward, Danny came home. As Teresa squeezed into a bleacher seat next to a balloon-toting child and several flag-waiving wives, she tried to make sense of her emotions. She was moments away from seeing Danny again and that reunion couldn't come soon enough. They had made a lot of mistakes during his time at home, and she was eager to make amends. But she was also overwhelmed by guilt. The ceremony was incomplete. Jennifer was supposed to be here with her, welcoming Rob home, not packing up the remnants of their life together and starting a new life as a widow.

Teresa's vision blurred with tears as she saw the soldiers march into formation, but as jubilant spouses rushed past her to greet the beaming soldiers, Teresa found her feet planted beneath her. She wanted desperately to run to Danny and to feel his arms around her, but the thought of Jennifer, and so many other Baumholder families for whom there would be no joyful reunion, made her feet feel leaden. By the time she reached Danny her face was streaked with tears, though if they were tears of joy or tears of sorrow, she simply could not say.

Meanwhile, Kristina was still waiting for Scott to get out of Iraq. His was one of the last companies to arrive in Iraq, which meant that they were also one of the last to leave. Finally, on a humid morning in late July, Scott called to tell her that he had arrived safely in Kuwait; she could stop worrying about him now. Kristina sat back and sighed in relief. Getting to Kuwait was almost as good as coming home; once Scott was there, it was only a matter of time. But only two hours later her relief was replaced by horror. The FRG had sent out a message announcing the deaths of two soldiers from the battalion. They had just been killed in a deadly traffic accident en route to Kuwait. She was stunned. This wasn't supposed to happen. The mission was over; no one was supposed to die now. Both of the deceased soldiers were married, and Kristina felt sickened by the thought of the anguish their wives must be feeling.

Two days later she heard from Scott again, and this time he

had found a web cam. Kristina was shocked by his appearance. He looked half dead; his eyes were nearly swollen shut with exhaustion and he looked even thinner than usual.

"You look awful!" she wrote. "What's going on?"

"I've been working for more than 48 hours straight trying to get the equipment ready for shipping," Scott explained.

"Why don't you go to bed?" she asked.

"I can't," he wrote back. "I've still got to get the trucks back. We've got to…"

Kristina waited for the conversation to continue, but minutes passed with no further communication and Scott's head had slipped out of view. He had fallen asleep mid-sentence.

Kristina barely slept the next few days, terrified that in his state of exhaustion Scott might fall victim to another deadly traffic accident. So it was an even greater relief when, a few days later, someone from the FRG called to tell her that the plane had left Kuwait and Scott would be in Baumholder the following morning.

This time, Kristina was determined to be ready. The FRG was telling people that they would call well in advance of the morning ceremony so that everyone would have time to prepare, but she wasn't taking any chances. Scott's last two homecomings had been a disaster; there was no way she was going to botch a third.

Her alarm woke her at 5 a.m. She showered and changed into the outfit she had chosen weeks earlier, straightened her long hair with a blow dryer, and applied and reapplied her make-up. She wanted to look perfect. Finally, at 7 a.m. the phone rang.

"Sorry I didn't call sooner," a woman from the FRG said. "I just found out that they are already here and the ceremony is going to be in about half an hour. I hope you were up."

Typical, Kristina thought, congratulating herself on beating fate this time. She finished dressing Marie and Tyler, grabbed the video camera and a diaper bag, and hurried to the car.

By the time she arrived at the gym Diane and her two sons were already waiting. The boys cuddled next to her, still half asleep, as Diane tried to keep still. After so many hurdles, so many setbacks, Thomas was finally coming home. Finally, they had the chance to get their marriage back on track. It had taken her 15 months to realize that it could all be gone in an instant, she thought, and she couldn't wait to start rebuilding what they had so nearly lost.

The crowd stomped and hollered as the soldiers marched into the gym. Diane found Thomas quickly and waived wildly as she saw him march into position. "Woo hoo!" she yelled, excitedly pointing him out to the boys.

Meanwhile, Kristina had been caught off guard by the sudden announcement that the ceremony was about to begin. As the crowd's applause thundered around her she struggled to turn on her video camera and point it at the soldiers while simultaneously holding up Marie to see. She couldn't find Scott at first; the soldiers all looked the same from where she stood. Then she spotted his lean gait and caught his eye. He was deeply tanned from his days in Kuwait, and he wore a huge smile on his browned face. Kristina's heart pounded violently and her hands shook so badly she was sure the video would be hopelessly blurred.

When the first sergeant yelled, "Dismissed!" Kristina lifted Tyler up in her free arm and dashed through the crowd. Just as Scott emerged from a throng of soldiers, Kristina noticed the music playing in the background: "Hero," by Mariah Carey. "And then a hero comes along, with the strength to carry on, and you cast your fears aside, and you know you can survive..." the pop diva crooned. Kristina couldn't imagine a more appropriate soundtrack for the reunion. We made it, she thought with astonishment. We really made it! She buried her face into Scott's shoulder and cried.

By the second week in August, all the rest of Baumholder's soldiers who were fortunate enough to survive the deployment would return home. One by one they would come marching into the Hall of Champions as their spouses felt their hearts thudding in their chests. One by one they would break from parade rest and rush forward, reaching out for babies who had become toddlers, children who had turned into pre-teens, and wives who had learned to be stronger and more independent than they had ever believed they could be. And one by one they would turn, head home, and try to remember how to be a family again. For the residents of Baumholder the long year of absence, which had dragged on for almost 15 months, was finally over.

EPILOGUE

Once again, Baumholder underwent a transformation. Music poured out of barracks room windows. Soldiers piled into the food court at lunch time, swelling lines to long-forgotten proportions. Hand-holding couples filled the downtown restaurants, lingering over drinks long after their empty plates had been cleared away. The local stores had their best months yet as soldiers blew through their considerable savings on new cars, stereos, and any other luxury items they could get their hands on.

It was a time of celebration, although not for everyone. Twenty-six Baumholder-based soldiers died during the deployment, some by hostile fire, some the victims of roadside bombs, some in accidents, and others by suicide. Many more were injured. For the families of these soldiers there was little consolation in seeing the rest of Baumholder's troops return. For them, the homecoming did not mark the end of a period of fear and loneliness but the beginning of a new, highly uncertain future that none of them had ever imagined or wanted.

Marriage was the other casualty of the deployment, though to a far lesser extent than many cynical Baumholder spouses had predicted. In the weeks after the homecoming, the post buzzed with rumors about jilted husbands. One soldier came home to find that his wife had cleared out their apartment, leaving behind a note explaining only that she didn't want to be with him anymore and had gone back to the States without him. Another soldier had been home for less than a week when he woke up one morning to find that his wife had disappeared, taking with her the entire contents of their bank account. Other troubled marriages limped along through stressful reunions, heading toward a likely divorce.[1]

Those were the sad stories of the deployment, but they were by no means the most common ones. For most families the first weeks and months after the homecoming were a time of jubilation and renewal, a point illustrated by a baby boom so large that Landstuhl hospital's OB/GYN clinic was forced to turn people away, overloaded by new pregnancies. Many residents in Baumholder have commented that the deployment changed their families in positive ways: they appreciate one another more, are grateful for whatever time they have together, and are better able to keep minor conflicts in perspective. As Jena noted, "One of the benefits of life in the military is that you get to keep having honeymoons."

Baumholder's soldiers and families were notified that the First Armored Division would return to Iraq in fall 2005. And so, the residents of Baumholder began taking advantage of their time together, hoping to be among the lucky ones who make it to a new post before stop loss/stop move puts them in the next round of deployment. They hope to take shelter, at least for a little while, with a unit that is not deploying in the near future. It is a fantasy that most will not realize. Even with the change of sovereignty in the summer of 2004 and the January 2005 democratic elections, the situation in Iraq remains precarious. Attacks against U.S. soldiers continue, along with a much broader scourge of violence against Iraqi civilians and the fledging police and military units. U.S. commanders have acknowledged that the United States will continue to require a sizeable presence in Iraq for years to come, and rotations into Iraq will continue for the foreseeable future. For those in the Army hoping to escape a second or even third deployment to Iraq, there are few safe havens. For the vast majority of the Baumholder community, the deployment of April 2003 to July 2004 is only the beginning.

For the women whose lives were followed in this book, the day their husbands returned home from Iraq was only the first step in a long road of trying to recover all that had been lost in the past 15 months. These are their stories.

KRISTINA

In the days leading up to Scott's arrival, Kristina had wondered how long their honeymoon period would last. She knew that it wouldn't last forever. The deployment had been hard on their marriage and they had a lot of issues to work through. But she hoped they would at least have a week or two of newly reunited happiness to get them off to the right start. That was not to be; before their first day together was through, it was clear to her that even her modest expectations were more than their strained marriage could deliver.

On Scott's first night at home they ordered dinner in from a local Italian restaurant. The deliveryman soon arrived with their order—a few entrées to share with the kids and some appetizers —and Scott handed Kristina $20 to pay the bill.

"Where's the rest?" Kristina asked.

"That's it," he replied. "Isn't that enough?"

Kristina looked at him incredulously.

"Of course it's not enough," she told him. She had asked him earlier if he had enough cash to pay for dinner and he had said he did. "How could you think that $20 would be enough to feed four people?"

"That's too expensive," Scott complained accusingly. "Don't you have any cash? Why didn't you plan better?" Kristina's face flushed with embarrassment as she broke open a piggy bank and counted out the rest of the bill in change. By the time they sat down to eat, the evening she had fantasized about for months had already been ruined.

The next day was even worse. Scott came home from reintegration training the following afternoon full of suspicion about what Kristina had done in his absence. He had spent the day sitting through mandatory lectures on responsible alcohol consumption and German driving laws but, preoccupied by tales of cheating wives some of the other soldiers had been passing off as the gospel truth, he had barely heard a word.

According to one rumor, wives in Baumholder left brooms on their porches and balconies to signal to boyfriends that their husbands were away and that they were available for sex. Variations of the ugly rumor spread from post to post during every deployment, but its ubiquity has never lessened its hold on credulous, suspicious listeners. Scott believed every word, and as soon as he came home he began searching for incriminating evidence. He went into the bathroom, opened up one of the cabinets above the sink, and there, toward the back on a top shelf, he found the proof he needed: an open pack of condoms. Examining the package with rising fury he set a trap, tossing the condoms onto the hallway floor, and waited to observe Kristina's telltale reaction when she found them.

Kristina walked by a few minutes later and picked up the condoms. "What are these doing here?" she asked casually.

"I was wondering the same thing," Scott replied with palpable hostility.

"Scott! These are yours!" Kristina shouted, stunned by the implied accusation. "We used them after Tyler was born. Don't you remember? God! Who did you think they belonged to?"

So we're back to this again, Kristina thought resentfully, remembering their awful reunion after Scott's deployment in Albania. She knew that he had asked around about her while he was deployed, checking with soldiers in the rear detachment to make sure that no one had seen her out at the local clubs. She had held her tongue while Scott was in Iraq, hoping that his jealously would fade in time, but this was too much. "You can either believe me or don't," she said dejectedly. "But there is no way that I can convince you." The fight dragged on for days, and with no end in sight Kristina finally told Scott, "Maybe we should go into counseling or something, because I don't know how much of this I can take."

Scott's reunion with the children was also strained. Tyler, overwrought by the sudden appearance of this near stranger, barely slept, and in his resulting exhaustion he cried and whined far more than usual. Scott often lost his patience, sending the toddler to his room as punishment. Kristina reminded Scott that Tyler was still a baby and unable to express himself. He cried because he needed something; there was no reason to punish him for that. "Fine," Scott said sullenly. "I'm just a dad. What do I have to say?"

While Tyler was uncomfortable in his father's presence, Marie was terrified that he might leave again. Each morning, as she watched her father start out the door dressed in the desert combat uniform he was still required to wear during the seven-day reintegration training, Marie became distraught, certain that he was going back to Iraq. "No, no, Marie," Scott said. "I'm not going to Iraq. I'm just going to work. I'll be back later today." Handing her the floppy, camouflaged hat that he had worn in Iraq, he told her that now that he was back in Baumholder, he didn't need that hat anymore. While he was home, he explained, he wore a black beret instead. "I can't go to Iraq without this hat," he said, stooping to her eye level. "I am giving it to you to keep for me. Unless I ask for it back, I am not going anywhere. Okay?" Marie smiled and nodded, clutching the hat tightly in her small fist.

The hat reassured Marie for a while, but her persistent questioning continued well into the fall months. "Is Daddy at big work or little work?" she asked Kristina any time Scott stayed away longer than expected. "He's only at little work," Kristina would assure her, promising that he would never go back to "big work"—Iraq—again. This time, Kristina had paperwork to back up her promise. In October, Scott signed a document that terminated his contract with the Army; by June, he would be a civilian.

The decision to leave the Army was a difficult one. Even though Scott had agreed months before he left Iraq to end his military career when his enlistment contract was up, he backed away from the decision as soon as he came home. With no college degree and little transferable work experience, he had few career prospects. Adding to the pressure, the Army had offered him a tantalizing $15,000 reenlistment bonus. He didn't want to stay in the Army, but he didn't see how he could afford to leave.

For Kristina, money wasn't the issue. They would muddle through somehow. But Scott had to get out of the Army. If he didn't, she was afraid it would be the end of their marriage. After weeks of fruitless discussions, she finally put her cards on the table.

"This isn't an ultimatum," she told Scott. "I'm not saying that if you reenlist I'm going to leave you. What I am saying is that if you deploy again, I'm not sure our family is going to make it."

As it was, she felt like she had lied to Marie for more than a year. She could not begin to imagine the loss of trust another absence would inflict. Scott and Tyler were only now beginning to form a relationship. How could they ever solidify that bond if he left again in a year or two? And as for her, even after months together Scott still seemed like a stranger. They barely communicated, and when they did it usually ended up in fight. They were hanging on by a thread. Another separation would surely destroy the tenuous connection that remained.

And so, realizing that his marriage was in jeopardy, Scott agreed to take his chances in civilian life. Today, Scott and Kristina are on their way to Oklahoma, where Scott has found a civilian job working with software and radar similar to that which he used in the Army. The transition into civilian life has been stressful, and between the anxiety of the move and caring for two small children, they have not had as much time to rebuild their relationship as Kristina thinks they need. Scott continues to insist they don't need marriage counseling, and while Kristina hopes the new location and stable work hours will help her family finally get past the upheaval of the deployment, she remains uneasy about the future of her marriage. Even after almost a year together, Kristina says, "Our family is still upside down."

BETH

The morning after Doug came home Beth rolled over and, observing her sleeping husband lying next to her, exclaimed groggily, "Oh! You're still here!" Even with Doug only inches away, she still could not quite trust that their reunion the previous afternoon had not been a dream.

Kathryn kept a close watch over her father during his first few weeks at home, eager for the time and attention he lavished on her. Doug could not get over how much energy it took to care for the three year old, nor just how loud she could be. Beth merely smiled knowingly, happily handing over parenting responsibilities a morning or an afternoon at a time. She and Doug quickly fell back into their old parenting routine, an easy transition Beth attributes to having maintained such good communication throughout the deployment.

After a relaxing, sun-drenched family vacation in Spain, Beth and Doug returned to normal life at warp speed. Beth's younger sister had come to live with them, and with only one car, Beth spent a good part of her days shuttling Doug, her sister, and Kathryn between work, school, swim practice, and various other engagements. In between taxi duties she took a part-time job tutoring soldiers and family members in mathematics. The extra money was a help with birthday and holiday expenses, but the real reason she took the job was, as she says, "to finally be able to use my brain." With her encouragement, Doug resumed his college studies and expects to finish a degree in business management within two years.

Soon after Doug came home, he made a shocking announcement. Not only did he want to stay in the military, he wanted to try out for Special Forces, an elite branch of the U.S. Army that takes part in highly specialized, covert operations. Beth was stunned. Doug had just come back from an extremely dangerous tour of duty; it was crazy to seek out even more dangerous assignments. But in time, Doug convinced her to consider it. True, he conceded, Special Forces units did take on dangerous missions, but they were highly trained, totally professional, and had the best equipment. They deployed frequently and durations varied, but he hoped his deployments would be no longer than a few months at a time. As a part of Special Forces, Doug hoped he would never miss a year or more of their lives at a time, and they could count on being in one place long enough to buy a house and put down roots. Reluctantly, Beth agreed that he should give it a try. "He's always been searching for that one thing that clicks for him," she explains with a sigh of resignation, "and so far, that's the military."

Beth has changed since Doug left for Iraq two summers ago. She is more confident in her role as a mother, more independent, and better prepared to be alone. The more time passes since the end of the deployment, the more her memories of the fear and anguish she suffered during it fade. "It's like childbirth," she laughs; it hurt a lot at the time, but now that it is over she can barely remember what the pain felt like. Even though Beth often feels uncomfortable about the way the Army is being used—her assessment of the war in Iraq ranges from ambivalence to outrage—her support of Doug's decision to stay in the Army is absolute. "I feel like if I made it through that I could make it through anything," she says confidently. And then she continues with somewhat less confidence, "It couldn't be that bad again, right?"

Doug sailed through Special Forces tryouts and today, the family is settling in to a new life in Ft. Bragg, North Carolina. Soon after leaving Baumholder, Beth and Doug were delighted to discover that she was pregnant.

JENA

In his first few weeks at home Jena barely let Adam out of her sight, following him around like a "puppy dog" and hanging on his every word. It was such a pleasure to be able to keep tabs on him, to watch him do mundane tasks like wash his hands or pour himself a drink. It was those little everyday actions that proved to her that he was really home, and she couldn't bear to miss a single one of them.

They used Adam's block leave to take a cruise in Mexico—a trip they had dreamed of for years—and spent time with their families back home in Alabama. Jena's grandmother passed away while they were there. Adam's commander granted him extra leave in order for him to stay for the funeral, a kindness for which Jena was profoundly grateful. She had endured much of her sorrow about her grandmother's illness on her own, and it was a tremendous consolation to have Adam's support when she needed it most.

Adam and Jena returned to their busy lives, he to work and she to her volunteer responsibilities with the FRG, and all too quickly, Jena found, she and Adam began taking their time together for granted. Ironically, it almost seemed as though they had communicated better when Adam was in Iraq than now that he was home. During the deployment everything else had stopped during his brief and sporadic phone calls, and for that small amount of time they'd had each other's undivided attention. Now they could be together whenever they wanted, but if they didn't set aside time for one another, days might pass without their ever really connecting. Jena and Adam have since settled the matter with a simple solution: As soon as Adam comes home from work, the next 30 minutes are their time—no television, no phone calls.

Now that they have settled back into their old routines, Jena says that she can see that the time apart changed them. Adam seems more "grown up" to her now, and she realizes that no matter how much time they spend talking about his 15 months in Iraq, they can never recover the time they lost. Jena has changed as well; she is more independent and self-assured. "Before Adam left all I wanted was to be Adam's wife," she says. "But now I take so much more pride in being me. I've learned to take pride in my own name."

Today, she and Adam remain committed to a life of military service, which Jena says is "one of those things that, if nobody does it, we're all in trouble." Adam has tentative orders to move to a different, stateside unit this August, but with the stop loss/stop move policy likely to go back into effect that same month, they assume that he will be forced to stay with his current unit in Baumholder for a second yearlong deployment to Iraq. For now, Jena says, she doesn't think about that possibility very much; she is too focused on enjoying the time she and Adam have to think about what she refers to blithely as "another vacation in the desert."

DIANE

Diane spent months worrying about the homecoming. She and Thomas had been through so much in their 15 months apart —a demoralizing professional setback, months of jealousy and suspicion, a near-divorce—and she knew that if their damaged marriage was going to survive, they were both going to have to be willing to work at it. Thomas's first few weeks at home led her to believe that there was reason to be hopeful.

Thomas seemed to have come back from Iraq with a renewed commitment to their marriage. He helped out around the house, washing the dishes, doing the laundry, and even picking up the kids after day care when Diane had errands to run. Following guidance once given to them by a chaplain, they made a conscious, daily effort to communicate better. They talked more, and instead of falling into their usual pattern of getting angry or offended and then letting the wounds fester until anger turned into rage, they sat down together and worked through the conflict.

Thomas's good intentions have stood the test of time. Almost one year after his homecoming, he continues to help Diane with the housework and child rearing, and they are working hard to get their marriage back on track. They still argue from time to time, still jangle each other's nerves on occasion, but they are taking it one day at a time and doing better than ever before in their 13 years of marriage. "Life sucks when the other person is gone," she says. "I know I can be on my own, but I don't want to be."

She will, however, soon be on her own again. Thomas was allowed to reenlist in the Army and is on orders to return to a unit in Fort Bragg that is currently deployed in Iraq. He will likely be sent to Iraq as soon as the family relocates this summer. Diane is anguished at the thought of what she describes as "another year in hell," but this time, she has far fewer worries about the toll the separation will take on her marriage. In some ways, she says, the deployment was the best thing that ever happened to her marriage. It forced them to take a hard look at their relationship and recommit to making it stronger. "We finally realized that we do want to be together," she says.

TASHA

On Anthony's first night at home, Tasha drew him a hot bath and sat beside the tub for hours while he soaked his tired limbs. "I am so sorry, baby," Anthony said over and over each time the conversation turned to the deployment. "I didn't want to have to put your through this."

"Stop apologizing!" she said. "You have nothing to be sorry for."

They ate dinner lying on the living room floor, unwilling to subject themselves to the formality of the dining room table.

Eventually, wrapped up in each other's arms, Anthony fell asleep, exhausted by the long trip home and 15 months of combat. He woke up with a start, full of apologies for ruining what was supposed to have been a romantic evening. Tasha hushed him gently. She had him safely in her arms now; there would be plenty of time for romance later.

Later that night Tasha felt Anthony's arm tighten around her waist. "Thank you, God," she heard him whisper softly. "She's really here." Tasha remained quiet, offering up her own silent prayer of thanks. She had been to enough memorial services and heard enough stories about marriages breaking up during the deployment to know that it didn't have to end this way.

Keisha traveled ahead of them to Anthony's next duty station, Fort Hood, Texas, staying with relatives while Tasha and Anthony tied up loose ends in Baumholder. Soon after their arrival in late summer 2004, they began building a new home in a community near Fort Hood, where they intend to remain for the rest of Anthony's Army career. The spacious home has rooms for everyone: Anthony and Tasha, Keisha, and Anthony's eight-year-old son from a previous marriage who, after a bitter custody dispute, moved in with them last fall.

As the months passed, Tasha noticed that her conversations with Anthony were increasingly full of uncomfortable silences. Anthony would "go off to his own world," playing computer games or just sitting and staring out the window wordlessly. "We never felt our marriage was in jeopardy, but our sanity was," Tasha said. Anthony agreed, and they went into counseling at their church's family life center. Today, Tasha and Anthony are no longer in marriage counseling, but they continue to attend family counseling sessions to help them adjust to their newly expanded family.

Tasha has different battles to face. Instead of wondering how she will get through a day filled with terror and isolation she is now absorbed in picking out drapes for their new home, completing an associate's degree in paralegal studies, and encouraging her unruly stepson to do his homework and eat his vegetables. Keisha is thriving at her new school. Anthony is safe, assigned to the rear detachment of a battalion that is currently deployed to

Iraq, and they hope that the timeline of rotations will keep him from returning to Iraq for at least another two years, though Tasha knows better than to count on that.

"This is a year I will never forget," she says of the deployment, though it has already started to seem like a blur. "I learned a lot about myself, about relationships, and about our country." She has learned that she is strong enough to love someone as fiercely as she loves Anthony and still survive without him. She has learned just how important the mother-daughter relationship she shares with Keisha is to them both. And she has learned that factors far outside of her control will continue to affect her future, at least as long as Anthony stays in the Army.

This is not the last deployment to Iraq that she and her family will face; of that she is certain. But, she hopes, the next time she will be better prepared. She will know what to expect, and friends and family in Texas will surround her, saving her from the isolation she experienced in Baumholder. She tries not to think about the likely possibility of future deployments. It is a part of being in the Army now, and there is nothing she can do to change that. "I'm not going to fight it," she says of Anthony's decision to stay in the Army until he gets his pension, seven years from now. "It's what he does."

The large television, which had been tuned to CNN every day that Anthony was deployed, is now tuned to different stations. Tasha no longer needs to know every minute of every day what the latest news in Baghdad is, or if another soldier has been killed by a roadside bomb. But the fact that her own husband is home now hasn't changed her prayers. "I still pray just as hard as I did when he was gone," she says, "because it is not over yet."

TERESA

This time, Teresa and Danny got their reunion right. There was no fighting, no yelling, no lashing out at one another for pain neither could control. Instead, they calmly, lovingly got to know one another again. They stayed in Europe during block leave, taking short trips to neighboring countries and enjoying the luxury of simply being together again, and by the end of the four weeks it almost seemed like Danny had never left.

But some things had changed. Danny's father had died just before he returned to Iraq. He and Teresa had attended the funeral, but had left California after only a few days so that Danny could prepare to return to his company. There had never been time to mourn, and even now that Danny is home, his father's death continues to be a subject he prefers not to discuss.

Jennifer, who had decided to stay in Baumholder until the soldiers returned, packed up her apartment and moved back to the States, alone. She is now enrolled in a graduate program in library science. Jennifer, Teresa, and Heather remain in frequent contact. Soon after Jennifer's departure, Heather and her husband also left Baumholder to move on to their next assignment. For Teresa, saying goodbye to Jennifer and Heather was almost like losing a part of herself. For more than a year they had been each other's lifelines, and now they were going their separate ways—one to another Army post with the man she loves, the other to a solitary future she had never planned for or predicted.

Danny understood how much Teresa had been through as a result of the deployment, and now that he was back it all came down to one question: Did she want him to get out of the Army? Teresa thought about it carefully. There had certainly been times she had wanted him to get out of the Army more than anything in the world, but now that he had returned safely she wasn't so sure. For all its sacrifices and challenges, the Army was home now, and Danny's dedication and loyalty to his fellow soldiers was one of the things Teresa admired most about him. They were a community, and she was a part of that too now. Walking away from the Army just wasn't a decision she felt ready to make, at least, not as long as Danny wanted to stay. "Just go to school," she said at last. He could stay in the Army as long as he wanted, but she wanted him to continue his education. That way, she said, he would be prepared if he ever decided to pursue a different career path and he would be around long enough to get to know his first child.

That was the other big change in their lives. Two months after Danny came home, the promise he had made to Teresa before he deployed—that they would be able to have children once he returned—was fulfilled. Teresa and Danny are expecting their first child in July. Danny was accepted into an Army-sponsored master's degree program in engineering and starts school this fall. Teresa and Danny remain ambivalent about his future career plans. Much about life in the civilian world is tempting—stability, safety, a higher salary—but with many of his peers leaving the Army, Danny feels a sense of duty not to abandon what increasingly feels like a sinking ship. For now, they are content to be in a safe, non-deployable assignment and together as they embark on their new role as parents.

NOTES

CHAPTER 3
1 Terry Boyd, "Baumholder Barracks Quieted by Deployments," *Stars and Stripes*, August 18, 2003

CHAPTER 4
1 Not her real name.
2 In order for Doug to be granted emergency leave and return to Baumholder, the company commander, battalion commander, and the brigade commander all had to recommend that he be redeployed. The final decision, however, would be made by the division commander, a position normally filled by a two star general.

3 Beth's assertion is supported by research. In a 1999 study by the RAND National Defense Research Institute, researchers reported that, "In a review of the literature concerning the effects of family factors on Army retention and readiness, Vernez and Zellman (1987) find relationships between perceptions of Army leadership and practice on the one hand, and well-being, commitment, retention, and job performance on the other. Similarly, the perception of Army support for one's family is an important predictor of outcome variables. For example, enlisted soldiers and officers who perceive that the Army is supportive of their families have fewer job problems and show a higher level of commitment to the Army (Burnham et al., 1992)."

Source: Colette Van Lamar, *Increasing a Sense of Community in the Military Family: The Role of Personnel Support Programs*, RAND National Defense Research Institute, 1999.

CHAPTER 5
1 Not his real name.

CHAPTER 6
1 Previously, four soldiers from Baumholder had been killed in Iraq in noncombat related incidents. Those soldiers were Pfc. Michael S. Adams, 20, of Spartanburg, S.C.; Sgt. Michael L. Tosto, 24, of Apex, N.C.; Pvt. Jason L. Deibler, 20, of Coeburn, Va.; and Pfc. Joseph P. Mayek 20, of Rock Springs, Wyo.

2 A field grade Article 15 is an administrative process carried out by the chain of command in lieu of a court martial. In this process, normally the battalion commander prefers the charges to the accused soldier, listens to any evidence or explanation, and makes a decision about guilt and possible punishment. The decision can be appealed to the next higher commander. The maximum allowable punishment for an NCO under a field grade Article 15 is reduction of one rank, forfeiture of half a month's base pay for two months (not including any special pay or allowances), and up to 45 days of extra duty and up to 60 days of restriction to unit area.

CHAPTER 7
1 Robert Schlesinger, "Army Reserve Battling an Exodus: War is seen as drain on ranks," *The Boston Globe*, November 23, 2003
2 Not her real name.

CHAPTER 8
1 Rick Scavetta, "USAREUR welcoming incoming R&R troops," *Stars and Stripes*, Sept. 26, 2003
2 Eligibility for the R&R program was determined by four categories. In order of priority, those categories were: 1. Soldiers who had an emergency leave situation (a serious family illness or surgery) that had not reached the high threshold for leave status during stop move/stop loss. 2. Soldiers whose wives had given birth during the deployment. 3. Soldiers who had been deployed or had served in Korea for at least six months out of a 12-month period. 4. All soldiers not undergoing unfavorable action. Soldiers in the first two categories were granted leave slots first, followed by soldiers in the third and fourth categories, whose order of priority was generally determined by lottery. Soldiers who were undergoing unfavorable action or were essential to meeting mission requirements were ineligible for leave.
3 According to Robert Strayhan, MD, a lieutenant colonel in the Air Force Reserve and practicing psychiatrist, frequent and extended absences test fledgling marriages at a time when they are not yet fully formed, making incidents of infidelity and jealousy more likely than they would be in better established relationships. He explains, "During the early phases of the relationship, physical attraction is most intense. Later, there is a settling period where the task is acceptance and compassionate growth. [Deployment] interrupts this process of moving from lust to love…so that when one wants the other partner so much physically, they aren't there. This phase of relationships can be more territorial and, for lack of a better word, jealous."

WINTER
1 Steve Liewer, Terry Boyd, and Kent Harris, "Holidays Lose Luster Without Deployed Dads," *Stars and Stripes*, December 24, 2003

CHAPTER 9

1 Terry Boyd, "In Germany, Saddam's Capture Sparks Hope for Loved Ones' Return," *Stars and Stripes*, December 15, 2003

2 According to psychologists, Jena's approach is central to successfully coping with a deployment, and is even more important for families with children. Col. Thomas G. Hardaway, M.D., writes in *Tips for Supporting the Child Whose Military Parent is Deploying*, "It is important that the family not put 'life on hold' in anticipation of the return of the deployed parent. This will result in stagnation, loss of direction, and burn-out." He recommends setting specific goals for both the remaining parent and the children to be completed before the return of the deployed spouse/parent.

CHAPTER 10

1 Soldiers were tasked with work in the tax center during the deployment in order to provide those soldiers who wished to file their taxes the opportunity to do so. Soldiers who preferred to delay filing their taxes until their return from Iraq received a deferment. Deployed soldiers were not taxed on military pay received during the mission, but they were still responsible for any taxes incurred due to other income sources or incurred during other nondeployment periods during the tax year.

CHAPTER 11

1 Terry Boyd, "Little Ones Make Room for Daddy," *Stars and Stripes*, January, 5, 2004

CHAPTER 12

1 Wiesbaden was home to another U.S. Army post in Germany. Soldiers based there were part of a different unit, and were on an earlier rotation schedule back from Iraq than soldiers from Baumholder.

2 Polish pottery was a must-have item for most women in Baumholder, along with German beer steins and antique sleds. Almost everyone in the room had her "own" pattern: a complete matching set of bowls, dishes, and serving platters.

SPRING

1 Robert Burns (Associated Press), "Length of Military's Stay in Iraq 'Unknowable,' Says Gen. Myers," *Stars and Stripes*, Feb. 20, 2004

CHAPTER 13

1 Ignacio Rubalcava, "Charlie 2-6 Soldiers Return Home," *Herald Union*, March 30, 2004. The *Herald Union* is the newspaper for the 104th ASG (Area Support Group) region of Germany.

CHAPTER 14
1 Rick Scavetta, Terry Boyd, and Jon Anderson, "Extending tours could be an option as U.S. faces uprisings," *Stars and Stripes*, April 9, 2004

CHAPTER 15
1 Col. Ralph A. Baker, commander of Baumholder's 2nd Brigade Combat Team, writing in the brigade newsletter, *The Striker Statement*, issue #46, May 25, 2004
2 The eight soldiers killed were: Staff Sgt. Esau G. Patterson Jr., 25, of Ridgeland, S.C.; Staff Sgt. Jeffrey F. Dayton, 27, of Caledonia, Miss..; Sgt. Ryan M. Campbell, 25, of Kirksville, Mo..; Spc. James L. Beckstrand, 27, of Escondido, Calif.; Spc. Justin B. Schmidt, 23, of Bradenton, Fla.; Pfc. Ryan E. Reed, 20, of Colorado Springs, Colo.; Pfc. Norman Darling, 29, of Middleboro, Mass.; and Pfc. Jeremy Ricardo Ewing, 22, of Miami, Fla.
Source: Kevin Dougherty, "Baumholder Reels from GIs' Deaths," *Stars and Stripes*, May 4, 2004
3 Kevin Dougherty, "Baumholder Reels from GIs' Deaths," *Stars and Stripes*, May 4, 2004

CHAPTER 16
1 Not her real name.

SUMMER, AGAIN
1 Eric Schmitt, "Its Recruitment Goals Pressing, the Army Will Ease Some Standards," *New York Times*, Oct. 1, 2004

EPILOGUE
1 Help was readily available for those who wanted it. Army Community Services sponsored weekend retreats for couples and group therapy sessions, and chaplains publicized their cell phone numbers, urging residents to contact them at the first sign of a problem.

ACKNOWLEDGMENTS

This book could not have been written without the candor of the brave women who told me their stories. I am profoundly grateful for their time and honesty. I am especially grateful to Jennifer Scheetz for her courageous willingness to allow me to make public her private tragedy.

Thanks to Staff Sgt. Mathew Leonard and Cpt. Ryan Bromenshenkl, who were so generous with their time, and to Lt. Col. Robert Strayhan, M.D., and Capt. Glen Wurglitz, PsyD for providing me valuable insights into the psychology of deployment.

Many thanks also to writers Sara Corbett and John Case, and to my agent, Daniel Greenberg, for their early encouragement, advice, and support.

For their belief in this book, I am tremendously appreciative of Karen Pavlicin, Tammy Price, and everyone else at Elva Resa Publishing. I am extremely grateful to my wonderful editor, Christy Lyon, for her careful reading and insightful comments. I could not have asked for a better editor.

I owe many thanks to my friends and family members for their faith in this book and the hours they spent serving as amateur editors, proofreaders, and gentle critics. Special thanks go out to my father, Corey Rosen, and my mother-in-law, Sally Redmond, for their enthusiasm and encouragement, my mother and step-father, Cynthia and Lynn Scott, and my father-in-law, Jeffrey Redmond. Special thanks to Alix Furness and Shawn P. O'Connor, who were two of my most thoughtful readers.

Most of all, I would like to thank my husband, Jon Redmond, whose patience, love, and unfailing support helped make this book possible.

BLUE STAR BANNER

The flag shown on the cover is known as the "service flag" or "blue star service banner." Soon after Baumholder's soldiers deployed to Iraq, these flags were ubiquitous on post.

Designed during WWI by Army Captain Robert Queissner, who at the time had two sons serving in the war, the flag soon became adopted as the symbol of military deployment. During World War II, the practice of displaying the service flag was widespread.

The blue star represents one family member serving. A banner can have up to five stars, signifying that five members of that family are currently in military uniform on active duty. The blue color represents hope and pride.

If the loved one dies while serving, a gold star of smaller size is superimposed over the blue star so that the blue forms a border. The gold color represents sacrifice to the cause of liberty and freedom.

The flag is an indoor flag, displayed in a window of the residence of the immediate family of the deployed service member. The service flag may also be displayed by an organization to honor the members of that organization serving in the Armed Forces during a period of war or hostilities.